JUST DESSERTS

THE CREATIVE COOKING SERIES

Every recipe in each of our cookbooks has been
kitchen tested by the author.

Susan Katz, co-author of *The Yogurt Book — 100 Ways to Use Yogurt Besides Eating It out of a Container,* has written and published several feature articles on a wide variety of topics for different national and local publications. She is an avid cooker and creator of recipes.

JUST DESSERTS

FAST BUT FANCY

SUSAN KATZ

A SPECTRUM BOOK

PRENTICE-HALL, INC., Englewood Cliffs, New Jersey 07632

Library of Congress Cataloging in Publication Data

Katz, Susan.
    Just desserts.

    (The Creative cooking series) (A Spectrum Book)
    Includes index.
    1. Desserts. I. Title. II. Series.
TX773.K33   641.8'6   77-26669
ISBN 0-13-514026-9
ISBN 0-13-514018-8 pbk.

Illustrations by Joyce Beigelisen

© 1978 by Prentice-Hall Inc.,
Englewood Cliffs, New Jersey 07632

A SPECTRUM BOOK

10 9 8 7 6 5 4 3 2 1

Printed in the United States of America

Prentice-Hall International, Inc., *London*
Prentice-Hall of Australia Pty. Limited, *Sydney*
Prentice-Hall of Canada, Ltd., *Toronto*
Prentice-Hall of India Private Limited, *New Delhi*
Prentice-Hall of Japan, Inc., *Tokyo*
Prentice-Hall of Southeast Asia Pte. Ltd., *Singapore*
Whitehall Books Limited, *Wellington, New Zealand*

CONTENTS

Many thanks to all those very special friends who went off their diets to help me taste and test these recipes, and who rummaged through their memories to come up with more desserts to try. And a particular "thank you" to Marcella Berti for typing, to Norma Karlin, and to Bob, who kept urging, "More chocolate, more chocolate."

INTRODUCTION

1

Dessert. The very word conjures up images of graceful towers of whipped-cream delights; chocolate fantasies of a definitely sinful nature; elaborate, melt-in-the-mouth confections almost too gorgeous to eat. "Dessert," unfortunately, is usually also accompanied by groans of dismay over the hours necessary to sculpt the perfect meringue or create the ultimate cheesecake, not to mention the panic and guilt felt over coming up with an end to the perfect meal that could easily have more calories — and less nutritional value — than the main course.

Just keep dreaming of gooey wonderfulnesses and forget about the rest. You don't have to spend all day in the kitchen. Elegant, easy, and best of all, fast desserts *can* be an integral part of every meal.

Each and every recipe was tested by the author (and some very indulgent friends) not only for taste but also for preparation time. You'll have to trust my judgment on the taste end of it (anything that wasn't super, but merely good, went out). The total time each recipe requires is given in the instructions — including how long the dessert has to cool, chill, freeze, bake, stand around, or what-have-you. Most of them can be made and served within fifteen minutes; others need up to a couple of hours fridge or freezer time.

No exotic ingredients or unusual cooking equipment is called for in these recipes. Whatever you have on hand or can easily get in the local supermarket is the basis for every dessert. Take pies, for example. In fourteen minutes, you can whip up a scrumptious Banana Split Pie (page 28) with nothing more complicated than a packaged crust, a couple of bananas, ice cream, and a few cherries. Practically instant, and incredibly delicious.

Baked Alaska (page 27) is a twelve-minute wonder every bit as delectable as any you've tasted anywhere. One mouthful and ice cream, as good as it is by itself, will never taste the same.

Fruit, whether fresh, frozen, or canned, is the magic ingredient that makes instant masterpieces out of ordinary foods. Start with a banana, add a little butter, a little sugar, and some rum, and with the flick of a match you have Bananas Flambée (page 57). It's the kind of dessert that impresses everyone with its elegance — and impresses you, the cook, with how fast and easy it is.

Mousse in the blender is a breeze (page 20), and it tastes so good you won't be able to believe it was so simple; puddings, custards, cakes — every kind of dessert — can be super-quick, super-easy, and super-delicious.

Finally, consider this bonus: every now and then, you can even make a whole meal of a dessert, in less time than it would probably take you to cook a main course alone.

DESSERTS CAN BE HEALTHY

Nutritionally, as part of a balanced meal, dessert very definitely has its place. Milk, for example, in some form or another, is a prime ingredient in many desserts. It's also the primary source of calcium and Vitamins A and D for most people. The adult daily requirement is sixteen ounces a day, but you don't have to drink it. Cheese, yogurt, ice cream, whipped cream — they're all acceptable alternatives to milk, and much more fun.

Fruits, essential ingredients in several fast and easy desserts, should be essential parts of everyone's diet. Oranges, strawberries, grapefruits, and tangerines are full of Vitamin C; apricots and apples, of Vitamin A. A fruit dessert not only tastes good, it's also good for you.

Cakes, pies, cookies, and the like, while perhaps calorically

on the heavy side, are good sources of protein, thiamine, niacin, riboflavin, and other nutrients in the bread and cereal group. You should have four daily servings of some sort of bread, cereal or other grain — like pasta, crackers, rice, and yes, even cakes, cookies, and pies.

Wherever possible, I have used only fresh ingredients or those with as few chemical additives as possible. Sugar is sugar, and no artificial sweeteners are recommended or included. Remember, desserts are meant to be taken in small doses, not huge helpings, and one small piece of chocolate cheese pie is not going to be the calorie that broke the scale's back.

One of the very nicest things about making desserts is using your imagination. None of the recipes here is really so hard and fast that you can't substitute one thing for another, or find shortcuts even shorter than mine. In fact, I've even suggested some ways of altering the recipes with just a slight change of ingredients. Strawberry shortcake becomes peach shortcake with barely a flick of the wrist; prune whip turns into apricot whip faster than you can blink an eye.

Got a couple of minutes? Make dessert. That's all you'll need to put a fabulous finish on a delicious dinner, without really even trying.

THE WELL-EQUIPPED KITCHEN

2

Even if you don't cook a lot, or elaborately, it seems safe to assume that your kitchen holds at least a reasonable assortment of basic cooking items: pots, pans, skillets, bowls of varying sizes, wooden spoons, a decent knife or two, and so on. Although that's about the most you'll need for any of these recipes, there are three basic pieces of equipment that will make desserting (and anything else) a real breeze.

ELECTRIC MIXER

Your electric mixer doesn't have to be terribly fancy (I got mine by opening up a bank account); a simple, lightweight hand model will do just fine, as none of the recipes calls for heavy batters or prolonged beating. Although some purists prefer wire whisks for beating air into egg whites or whipped cream, nothing beats an electric mixer for speed. Second best is a rotary beater, which requires a little more hand action but still cuts time considerably. For most of these recipes, except where specifically indicated, the gourmet's wire whisk runs a poor third. It's an invaluable kitchen tool, but not when you're in a hurry.

BLENDER

There is practically nothing a blender can't do, from making crumbs to chopping nuts to combining a bunch of ingredients in minutes. Of course, you can do by hand anything a blender can do, but it takes a lot longer and you work a lot harder. An electric mixer can do some of a blender's work, but not all, and once you've discovered how much easier life is with a blender *and* a mixer, you'll wonder how you ever lived without them.

DOUBLE BOILER

A double boiler is nothing more than two pots and a cover, the top pot sitting firmly balanced in the bottom one. The two can be used separately, of course (the top fits both); but when they are fitted together, the bottom holds water at a boil or a simmer, while the ingredients that must be melted or cooked over indirect heat sit in the top. If you don't want to buy a double boiler (the five-and-dime is a good source), you can use a smaller pot that fits comfortably into a larger one. If it's a little off-balance, that won't matter much; the main thing is that the water in the bottom pot should just barely touch the underside of the top pot. (If there's too much water, it will spill out over the sides.)

STOCKING YOUR CUPBOARDS AND REFRIGERATOR

The recipes in this book call for, in general, things you usually have around: eggs, milk, sugar, butter or margarine, flour, and the like, but you might like to stock up on a few specific things against dessert emergencies:

Frozen fruit (the quick-thaw kind, or plain, unsweetened)
Frozen pie crusts (almost indistinguishable from homemade)
Frozen pound cake, spongecake, angel food cake

Ice cream and sherbet
Assorted jams, jellies, and preserves
Prepared graham-cracker crusts
A variety of instant puddings and pie fillings
Various fruit-flavored gelatins; unflavored gelatin
Ladyfingers
Graham crackers
Vanilla and chocolate wafers
Canned fruit or pie fillings
Nuts, raisins, coconut
Refrigerator rolls: buttermilk, crescent, cinnamon

Some other things you might need but shouldn't keep for more than a week in the refrigerator:

Cottage, ricotta, and cream cheese
Heavy cream
Yogurt
Packaged cake

If you're at all organized, the easiest thing to do is to decide in advance what kind of desserts you want to make and fill in accordingly. If organization is not your strong point, a quick trip to the supermarket or substituting something you do have on hand for something you don't is the answer.

PUDDINGS, MOUSSES, AND CUSTARDS

3

Nothing provides quite the same taste treat for the tongue as a creamy spoonful of custard, a light and airy mousse, or a smooth and tasty pudding. You can serve custards and puddings warm or cold; mousse is usually either chilled or frozen. Technically, some of the desserts in this chapter are none of these, but whether they're called "whips," "snows," or anything else, they're still fast, easy, and scrumptious.

My favorite is the first recipe, Quick Custard, for two reasons. It tastes terrific, especially over some fresh, juicy strawberries, and it really is simple. My next favorite is the Easy Blender Mousse (page 20), for the same reasons and also because it proves that gourmet cooking doesn't have to be a long, involved, many-step process.

These are not among the most low-calorie desserts, but as so many of them use fresh fruit, it's easy to keep the sugar content down, especially if you prefer food on the tart side. Of course, whipped cream is not exactly diet food, but these are so good they're worth every calorie.

COOKING HINTS

Always use a double boiler with hot, not boiling, water to make custards or melt chocolate. If the water is too hot, the egg whites will separate from the yolks, and although the custard will still be edible, it won't look very pretty.

When you're beating egg whites till "stiff, but not dry,"

start with them at room temperature and beat at medium speed until the beater leaves tracks in the whites. When you pick the blades up, the whites should stand in peaks and look shiny.

If a recipe calls for yolks only, you can store the leftover whites in the refrigerator for up to four days or in the freezer for several months. Yolks can also be stored in the refrigerator for three or four days, or frozen, adding salt (if they are going to be used in cooking) or sugar (if they are destined for baked or sweet foods) to stabilize them and keep them from becoming pasty. Both whites and yolks should be thawed in the refrigerator for 8 to 10 hours or at room temperature for 5 to 6 hours.

Melt chocolate over hot water in a double boiler to prevent scorching. Grating chocolate is easier if the chocolate is cold; shaving it or making chocolate curls is a simple job if the chocolate is slightly warm.

If you have no time to purée fresh or frozen fruit for a recipe, substitute puréed baby food.

QUICK CUSTARD

2 egg yolks
2 teaspoons curaçao
2 tablespoons sugar

Mix all ingredients in top of double boiler. Set over simmering water and beat, with a wire whisk, until thick and hot. Serve warm, as is, or over fresh strawberries or other fruit. (Make sure the water is not boiling, or the custard will curdle.)

Serves 2. About 156 calories per serving.
Start to serve time: 10 minutes.

Increase each ingredient proportionately for each additional mouth. If you make a little extra, I can guarantee it won't be left over.

APPLE "PUDDING"

6 slices whole wheat
  bread
6 tablespoons melted
  butter or margarine
1/2 cup sugar
1/2 teaspoon
  cinnamon
1/4 cup finely
  chopped nuts
1 pound applesauce
1/3 cup raisins
1/4 cup maple syrup

Trim crusts from bread; dip each slice into melted butter or margarine, then into a mixture of sugar, cinnamon, and nuts. Put two slices of bread in the bottom of a small baking dish; top with applesauce; sprinkle with raisins. Repeat layers, ending with bread. Pour maple syrup over all and bake half an hour, or until golden brown.

Serves 6. 355 calories per serving.
Start to serve time: about 40 minutes.

I'm not sure whether this is cake or pudding, just that it's yummy. You can make it for yourself alone with two slices of bread (cut each one into three strips so you can make three layers of two strips each) and proportionately less of the other ingredients. Bake on a small pie tin.

APPLE SNOW

1 cup granulated sugar
2 large, tart apples,
  peeled and cored
4 egg whites
dash of salt

Put sugar into a large bowl and grate the apples directly onto it. Stir until dissolved. Add egg whites and salt, and beat until stiff. Serve immediately or chill, if desired.

Serves 8. 154 calories per serving.
Start to serve time: 15 minutes.

APPLESAUCE MOUSSE

1 pound applesauce,
  homemade, jarred,
  or canned
  (unsweetened)
1/2 cup sugar
1 tablespoon lemon
  juice
1/8 teaspoon
  cinnamon
dash of salt
1/2 teaspoon vanilla
  or almond extract
1 cup heavy cream,
  whipped

Dissolve sugar in applesauce; add lemon juice, cinnamon, salt and extract. Fold into whipped cream. Chill thoroughly before serving, or freeze until firm, about 2 hours.

Serves 6. 254 calories per serving.

Preparation time: 10 minutes; Chill time: 1 hour or longer.

APRICOT WHIP

1 cup dried apricots
1 cup milk
1/4 cup milk
1/4 lemon
1/2 cup sugar
2 egg whites

Soak the apricots in 1 cup of milk at least half an hour. Put them with the additional 1/4 cup milk, lemon (peel and all), and sugar into the blender, and blend at high speed until smooth. Beat egg whites until stiff (you can do this while the apricots are soaking); fold in the apricot mixture and chill (don't freeze).

Serves 6. About 157 calories per serving.

Preparation time: 35 minutes; Chill time: The longer the better.

This is like a wonderful mousse and tastes better the colder it is. Try it with other dried fruits or use puréed baby fruits —pears, peaches, prunes—and about 3/4 cup milk total. (If you use purée, you don't need the blender; just mix well to dissolve sugar, add a little lemon juice, and grate in some lemon peel.)

CANDY BAR MOUSSE

8 1-oz. milk chocolate bars with almonds
1/4 cup water
2 eggs, well beaten
1 cup heavy cream, whipped

Break up the candy bars and combine with water in top of double boiler. Heat until melted. Remove from heat; add eggs, beating constantly. Put back over hot water and cook about 2 minutes, stirring, until thick. Cool slightly; fold into whipped cream. Chill thoroughly, or freeze about 1 hour before serving.

Serves 6. About 390 calories per serving.
Preparation time: 12 minutes; Chill time: At least 1 hour.

This is very, very sweet. You might try substituting semi-sweet or bittersweet chocolate bars (the candy, not cooking chocolate) instead. You could also try it without the nuts, but the texture is nice with them.

COFFEEMALLOW MOUSSE

16 marshmallows, cut in quarters
3/4 cup hot coffee
pinch of salt
1/4 teaspoon vanilla
1 cup heavy cream, whipped
1/4 cup walnuts

Cook marshmallows with coffee over low heat until marshmallows are dissolved. Cool, then add salt and vanilla. Fold into whipped cream alternately with chopped nuts. Chill.

Serves 8. 196 calories per serving.
Preparation time: 15 minutes; Chill time: 1 hour or more.

CRÈME BRULÉE

1 cup heavy cream
2 egg yolks
3 tablespoons brown sugar

Bring cream to a boil in a heavy saucepan. Beat the egg yolks until they are lemony, and add hot cream to them, a little at a time, beating until the mixture is thoroughly blended. (If you add the hot cream all at once, the eggs will begin to cook, and you'll have a mess.) Cook over medium heat, stirring, until the mixture is thick enough to coat a wooden spoon. Pour into a greased 10-inch pie pan, and chill until just before ready to serve.

When ready to serve, preheat the broiler. Sprinkle the top of the cream with brown sugar; place under the broiler until glazed.

Serves 4. 275 calories per serving.
Start to serve time: 15 minutes.

This is one of the most elegant and easy desserts to make. Of the several variations, and everyone seems to have a favorite recipe, this one has worked best for me.

CUSTARD, ITALIAN STYLE

6 egg yolks
6 tablespoons sugar
9 tablespoons Marsala

Combine all ingredients in top of double boiler and whip with wire whisk until heavy and thick, about 5 to 10 minutes. Serve warm.

Serves 4. About 185 calories per serving.
Start to serve time: 5-10 minutes.

This is delicious cold, too. If you like, you can serve it over fresh fruit, but I think it's best on its own.

EASY BLENDER MOUSSE

*1 6-oz. package
semi-sweet chocolate
morsels or 6-oz.
semi-sweet
chocolate, broken
into small pieces
5 tablespoons hot
water
2 tablespoons cognac
4 eggs, separated*

In a blender, at high speed, blend chocolate for about 8 seconds or until grated. Add hot water and blend again at high speed for another 8 or 10 seconds. Add cognac; blend for 5 seconds. Add egg yolks; blend until everything is very well combined.

Beat egg whites until stiff. Fold in chocolate mixture gently. Chill.

Serves 4. 305 calories per serving.
Preparation time: 7 minutes; Chill time: 1/2 hour or longer.

I have made this so often I can almost do it blindfolded. It works every time. Instead of cognac, you can use strong coffee, rum, orange liqueur, or in a pinch, orange juice and one teaspoon vanilla.

FRUIT WHIP

*1 cup applesauce
1 cup heavy cream,
whipped
1 tablespoon grated
orange peel
1 cup fresh
strawberries*

Combine applesauce, whipped cream, and orange peel. Gently fold in strawberries and serve.

Serves 4. About 300 calories per serving.
Start to serve time: 6 minutes.

If you don't have strawberries, try orange sections or almost any other whole fruit. It's nice to find something to bite into.

PEACHY KEEN MOUSSE

1 cup canned peaches,
well drained (reserve
1 cup of syrup)
1 cup peach syrup,
heated until boiling
1 package orange
gelatin
1/4 cup heavy cream
dash of salt
1/4 cup Marsala

Purée peaches in blender until smooth. Dissolve gelatin in hot peach syrup; add to purée and blend. Add cream; blend again. Add salt and Marsala; blend till smooth. Pour into serving bowl and chill until ready to serve. Top with whipped cream and sprinkle with cinnamon, if desired.

Serves 4. About 250 calories per serving.

Preparation time: 8 minutes; Chill time: 1 hour or more.

PRUNE WHIP I

1-1/2 cups pitted
cooked prunes
1/4 cup confectioners'
sugar
1/2 teaspoon grated
lemon peel
1 cup heavy cream,
whipped

Purée prunes in blender, adding sugar a little at a time until well mixed and smooth. Add lemon peel and blend again. Fold prune mixture into whipped cream and refrigerate until thoroughly chilled.

Serves 6. About 300 calories per serving.

Preparation time: 8 minutes; Chill time: 1 hour or more.

PRUNE WHIP II

*1-1/2 cups pitted
 cooked prunes
2 teaspoons lemon
 juice
2 egg whites
dash of salt
2 tablespoons sugar*

Purée prunes in blender; add lemon juice. Beat egg whites until foamy; add sugar and salt and beat until stiff peaks form. Add prune purée, a little at a time, beating well after each addition. Beat at high speed about 2 minutes longer. Chill.

Serves 6. About 75 calories per serving.

Preparation time: 10 minutes; Chill time: 1 hour or more.

This is much lighter and much lower in calories than Prune Whip I, but it tastes wonderful. An easier method, for either, is to use a jar of cooked prunes that you drain and pit. If prunes are not your thing, try canned peaches, apricots, pears, or crushed pineapple. Just remember to drain the syrup off well.

SOUFFLÉ À L'ORANGE

*1/4 cup orange
 marmalade
1 teaspoon lemon
 juice
1 egg white
dash of salt
1 tablespoon sugar
2 tablespoons chopped
 walnuts*

Preheat the oven to 350°F.

Heat marmalade with lemon juice until melted; set aside.

Beat egg white with salt until soft peaks form; gradually add sugar and beat until dissolved and stiff peaks form. Fold in marmalade mixture.

Spoon into two heatproof dishes (small ones); sprinkle with chopped nuts. Bake 15 minutes or until golden. Serve immediately, or the soufflé will collapse.

Serves 2. 75 calories per serving.

Start to serve time: 20 minutes.

SURPRISE, SURPRISE

*1-1/2 cups crushed
   chocolate sandwich
   cookies
1 cup sugar
1/2 cup light cream or
   half-and-half
1-1/2 cups heavy
   cream, whipped
1/4 cup brandy*

Mix cookies (don't crush them too fine, as it's the texture as well as the taste that counts), sugar, and light cream or half-and-half together. Fold into whipped cream until well blended. Add brandy and mix thoroughly, but gently. Refrigerate about 15 minutes before serving.

Serves 4. About 575 calories per serving.
Preparation time: 7 minutes; Chill time: 15 minutes or longer.

Needless to say, this is rather rich, but it is very good. You can substitute vanilla wafers and 1/4 teaspoon almond extract for the chocolate cookies.

ICE CREAM, SHERBET, AND YOGURT DESSERTS

4

A little imagination can turn good old ice cream — and there's nothing bad about that — into a spectacular creation that looks as if you've been toiling in the kitchen for hours instead of minutes. If you're so inclined, you can make your own ice cream, without churning or beating. It may not be the most classic form, but the taste and texture are superb.

Many of the recipes here should be made before you start dinner, to allow enough freezing or chilling time — at least one hour, usually more — before they are eaten. As they're not at all complicated, the initial preparation shouldn't take more than a few minutes. Read over the recipes first and plan ahead; they're deliciously worth the trouble.

Ice cream and yogurt, by the way, are considered to be reasonable substitutes for part of your daily milk requirement. Half a cup of ice cream is equal to one-quarter of a cup of milk; yogurt has the same nutritional value as milk, ounce for ounce.

COOKING HINTS

When you're beating cream for frozen desserts, beat it only till soft peaks form, or it will be too buttery.

Too much sugar in a recipe will prevent freezing; if you don't think a recipe is sweet enough for you, try another one.

To unmold frozen desserts, dip them briefly into hot water,

invert a plate on top of the mold, and turn the whole thing upside down, with the plate resting on the palm of your hand.

If you want to give yogurt a stiffer texture, fold it into a stiffly beaten egg white.

BAKED ALASKA

1 10-inch sponge cake
1 quart any flavor ice
  cream, slightly soft
4 egg whites
pinch of salt
1/4 cup confectioners
  sugar
1 teaspoon vanilla

Preheat oven to 450° F.

Slice sponge cake into two layers (save one slice for another dessert), and cover cake with ice cream, almost to the edge. Beat egg whites with salt until stiff; add sugar, a little at a time; flavor with vanilla. Cover ice cream completely with meringue. Bake for 5 or 6 minutes, or until meringue begins to brown. Serve immediately.

Serves 10. About 143 calories per serving.
Start to serve time: 15 minutes.

BANANAS À L'ORANGE

1 banana, peeled
1 tablespoon butter,
  melted
1/4 cup brown sugar,
  firmly packed
1 teaspoon grated
  orange rind
1 teaspoon cinnamon
2 scoops vanilla ice
  cream

Cut banana in half lengthwise, then crosswise. Arrange in baking dish and pour melted butter on top. Mix sugar, orange rind, and cinnamon together; sprinkle over bananas. Broil about 3 minutes, until glazed. Serve over ice cream.

Serves 2. About 350 calories per serving.
Start to serve time: 7 minutes.

BANANA "ICE CREAM"

4 very ripe bananas
1/2 cup heavy cream

Peel and freeze bananas. (Freezing takes a couple of hours, but you can do it days before.) When ready to use, cut up bananas and chop in blender till mashed. Whip cream and fold in. Freeze until firm; about an hour.

Serves 4. About 184 calories per serving.
Preparation time: 5 minutes; Freeze time: 2 hours or more.

If you always thought homemade ice cream meant hours of churning, guess again. This may not be the traditional method, but in taste and consistency, it's a winner.

BANANA SPLIT PIE

1 9-inch graham
   cracker crust
1 pint vanilla ice
   cream, slightly
   softened
1 large banana
1 21-oz. can sweet
   dark cherries, well
   drained

Spread ice cream in crust. Slice banana diagonally; arrange on top of ice cream and spoon cherries on top. Serve immediately or freeze until ready.

Serves 6. About 340 calories per serving.
Start to serve time: 12 minutes.

BERRY BERRY YOGURT

1 cup yogurt
1/4 cup honey
1/4 cup any berries

Blend all ingredients in the blender. Chill; serve over more berries or plain pound cake sprinkled with a little rum or brandy.

Serves 2. About 190 calories per serving.
Preparation time: 5 minutes; Chill time: 15 minutes or more.

BOURBON STREET PARFAIT

16 ladyfingers
1/4 cup bourbon
1 cup applesauce
1/4 cup strawberry
  preserves
1 cup heavy cream,
  whipped

Arrange 2 ladyfingers in each of 8 individual serving dishes; sprinkle with bourbon. Combine applesauce and preserves; fold into whipped cream. Put about 1/3 cup of applesauce mixture into each dish.

Serves 8. About 330 calories per serving.

Start to serve time: 10 minutes.

CHEESE FREEZE

1-1/2 cups cottage or
  ricotta cheese
1/2 cup sugar
1 teaspoon vanilla
1 egg
2 pints vanilla ice
  cream, slightly
  softened

Blend cottage or ricotta cheese with sugar, vanilla, and egg in blender, till smooth. Add to ice cream and beat with electric mixer until well mixed. Pour into loaf pan; cover with foil; freeze until firm.

Serves 8. About 235 calories per serving.

Preparation time: 10 minutes; Freeze time: 2 hours.

CHOCOLATE ICE CREAM PIE

1 9-inch graham
  cracker crust
2 squares semi-sweet
  chocolate, melted
1/2 cup butter or
  margarine, softened
2 eggs
3/4 cup sugar
1/2 teaspoon vanilla
1 pint butter-almond
  ice cream

Put all ingredients, except ice cream and pie crust, in blender and blend until smooth, or beat well with an electric mixer. Pour into crust and chill until thoroughly cooled. Just before serving, spoon softened ice cream on top.

Serves 8. About 316 calories per serving.

Preparation time: 10 minutes; Chill time: 1 hour or longer.

COFFEE PARFAIT

1 cup heavy cream
2 tablespoons sugar
2 tablespoons cognac
1 quart coffee ice
cream
instant coffee granules

Whip cream with sugar and cognac. Place a scoop of ice cream in each serving dish; sprinkle with powdered coffee; top with whipped cream; sprinkle with a little more instant coffee.

Serves 8. About 264 calories per serving.

Start to serve time: 10 minutes.

CREAM FREEZE

1-1/2 cups heavy
cream, whipped
6 egg yolks
1/2 cup sugar
1 teaspoon almond
extract

Beat egg yolks and sugar till thick and lemon-colored; beat in almond extract. Fold in whipped cream; pour into square pan; freeze until firm.

Serves 12. About 160 calories per serving.

Preparation time: 10 minutes; Freeze time: 2 hours or more.

EASY ICE CREAM CAKE

1 small angel food
cake
1 pint peach ice
cream
fresh or canned
peaches, sliced
1 cup heavy cream
4 tablespoons sugar
1 teaspoon vanilla

Slice cake in half horizontally. Spread ice cream over one half; top with peach slices, reserving some for decoration. Cover with top half of cake. Whip cream with sugar and vanilla; spread over cake. Decorate with reserved peaches.

Serves 10-12. About 200 calories per serving.

Start to serve time: 8 minutes.

This can be varied according to whatever flavor ice cream you like best, with a complementary fruit or chopped nuts. Instead of whipped cream, try any of the sauces in Chapter 9.

FLAMING FRUIT AND ICE CREAM

*2 10-oz. packages
  frozen peaches
2 tablespoons brown
  sugar
1/4 cup peach or
  apricot brandy
1/4 cup warm brandy
1 quart ice cream,
  peach or vanilla*

Drain peaches, sprinkle with sugar. Put in casserole and sprinkle with brandy. Let stand until ready to serve. Just before serving, heat brandy and pour over peaches. Ignite; pour over ice cream.

Serves 6–8. About 350 calories per serving.

Start to serve time: 10 minutes.

FROZEN CHEESE DESSERT

*2 cups cottage cheese
3 cups sour cream
2 cups confectioners
  sugar
1 teaspoon vanilla*

Combine all ingredients in blender until smooth. Refrigerate for immediate use, or freeze for future. Top with preserves if desired.

Serves 8. About 300 calories per serving.

Start to serve time: 10 minutes.

FROZEN SHERBET PIE

*1 9-inch graham
  cracker crust
1-1/2 pints lemon
  sherbet
2 8½-oz. cans crushed
  pineapple
2 tablespoons
  cornstarch*

Freeze crust for 10 minutes; fill with sherbet. Put in freezer until after next step. Drain pineapple, saving 2 tablespoons juice. Combine pineapple, juice, and cornstarch in saucepan; cook, stirring, until thickened. Let cool and spread on top of sherbet. Freeze until firm.

Serves 8. About 250 calories per serving.

Preparation time: 20 minutes; Freeze time: 1 hour.

GRASSHOPPER PIE

24 chocolate creme sandwich cookies, finely crushed
1/4 cup melted butter
1/4 cup crème de mênthe
1 pint softened vanilla ice cream
2 cups heavy cream, whipped

Combine all but 1/2 cup crumbs with butter and press into buttered 9-inch spring-form pan. Set aside.

Fold whipped cream and crème de mênthe into ice cream; pour into pan. Sprinkle with reserved crumbs, freeze until firm.

Serves 10. About 380 calories per serving.

Preparation time: 15 minutes; Freeze time: 2 hours.

There are a lot of variations on this recipe, and everyone who has one claims it as The Authentic one.

ICE CREAM MOLD

1 quart vanilla ice cream
1 quart strawberry ice cream

Line a medium-sized ring mold with vanilla ice cream, about 1/2 inch thick. Fill the center in with strawberry ice cream, and let freeze until firm. Unmold and serve garnished with fresh strawberries. Any two flavors of ice cream or of ice cream and sherbet will work.

Serves 8. About 264 calories per serving.

Preparation time: 5 minutes; Freeze time: 1 hour.

LEMON ICE CREAM

2 cups heavy cream
1 cup sugar
2 tablespoons grated lemon peel
1/3 cup lemon juice

Mix sugar and cream together until sugar is dissolved. Mix in lemon peel and juice. Pour into square pan or individual serving dishes and freeze until firm.

Serves 6. About 300 calories per serving.

Preparation time: 5 minutes; Freeze time: 2 hours or more.

MELON MELBA

2 cups cantaloupe,
  cubed
2 cups honeydew,
  cubed
2 cups watermelon,
  cubed
1 10-oz. package
  frozen raspberries,
  thawed, puréed, and
  strained
1 pint vanilla ice
  cream

Mix melon cubes with raspberries; refrigerate until ready to serve. To serve, scoop ice cream into individual serving dishes; top with melon/melba mixture.

Serves 6. About 180 calories per serving.

Start to serve time: 10 minutes.

NUTSY ICE CREAM PIE

1 9-inch graham
  cracker crust
1 quart vanilla ice
  cream, softened
1/3 cup chunky
  peanut butter
1/2 cup honey
3/4 cup peanut
  brittle, crushed

Spoon half the ice cream into pie crust. Mix peanut butter and honey together until smooth; spoon half the mixture over ice cream and sprinkle with half the peanut brittle. Repeat the layers. Freeze until firm.

Serves 10. About 420 calories per serving.

Preparation time: 15 minutes; Freeze time: 2 hours or more.

PEARS HÉLÈNE

4 pear halves
4 scoops vanilla ice
  cream
1/2 cup chocolate
  syrup
1 tablespoon orange
  liqueur

Place each pear half in a dish; top with a scoop of ice cream. Mix chocolate syrup and liqueur together in small pan; heat through. Pour over ice cream and serve.

Serves 4. About 300 calories per serving.

Start to serve time: 6 minutes.

PEACHES "ROMANOFF"

1 pint peach ice
  cream
2 fresh peaches,
  sliced
1 tablespoon sugar
8 crushed macaroons
peach brandy

Put ice cream in four individual serving dishes; cover with sliced peaches. Mix sugar and macaroons; sprinkle over each; spoon a little brandy over all.

Serves 4. About 300 calories per serving.

Start to serve time: 5 minutes.

RASPBERRY ICE CREAM

1 cup heavy cream,
  whipped
2/3 cup sweetened
  condensed milk
1 tablespoon lemon
  juice
1 10-oz. package
  frozen raspberries,
  partially thawed

Blend everything but whipped cream together until smooth; fold into whipped cream. Freeze in refrigerator tray until firm.

Serves 8. About 222 calories per serving.

Preparation time: 10 minutes; Freeze time: 2 hours.

RED, WHITE, AND BLUE PARFAIT

1 pint raspberry
  sherbet
1 pint lemon sherbet
1 cup honeydew, cut
  into chunks
1 cup cantaloupe, cut
  into chunks
1/4 cup blueberries

Layer 1/4 of the raspberry sherbet, 1/4 of the melon chunks, and 1/4 of the lemon sherbet into each of 4 parfait glasses. Top with blueberries.

Serves 4. About 320 calories per serving.

Start to serve time: 10 minutes.

SPEEDY YOGURT SUNDAE

2 apples, cored
2 bananas, sliced in
half lengthwise
2 cups yogurt, plain
or flavored
1/4 cup chopped
walnuts
1/4 cup raisins

Quarter apples, but do not peel. Blend at high speed in blender until very smooth. Place half a banana in each of four dessert dishes, top with 1/4 the blended apples and half a cup of yogurt, and sprinkle with nuts and raisins.

Serves 4. About 249 calories per serving.

Start to serve time: 7 minutes.

STRAWBERRY/ALMOND YOGURT

1 cup plain yogurt
1/3 cup sugar
2 teaspoons vanilla
extract
2 teaspoons almond
extract
2 pints strawberries

Mix all ingredients together. Chill until ready to serve.

Serves 4. About 143 calories per serving.

Preparation time: 5 minutes; Chill time: 15 minutes or more.

Any berry will substitute nicely here, as will apples, peaches, bananas, or almost any fresh fruit in season.

STRAWBERRIES MARNIER

4 oz. Grand Marnier
1 pint vanilla ice
cream, slightly
softened
2 pints strawberries,
washed

With a fork, blend Grand Marnier and ice cream until creamy. Spoon over fresh strawberries.

Serves 4. About 210 calories per serving.

Start to serve time: 5 minutes.

STRAWBERRIES 'N YOGURT PARFAIT

2 cups yogurt, plain
2 teaspoons vanilla
2 cups sliced
   strawberries
2 tablespoons sugar
4 oranges, peeled and
   sectioned

Put yogurt, vanilla, strawberries, and sugar in blender; blend until smooth. Spoon into six parfait glasses, alternating with orange slices. Chill until firm.

Serves 6. About 150 calories per serving.

Start to serve time: 10 minutes.

TUTTI-FRUTTI

1 quart vanilla ice
   cream
1 cup mixed candied
   fruit, chopped
4 tablespoons heated
   maple syrup

Place a scoop of ice cream in each of four serving dishes; top with about 1/4 cup chopped candied fruit and a tablespoon of hot maple syrup.

Serves 4. About 494 calories per serving.

Start to serve time: 5 minutes.

VERY SPECIAL ICE CREAM CAKE

1/2 cup sugar
1/2 cup water
1/2 cup dark rum
1 large sponge cake
1 pint vanilla ice
   cream
1 pint raspberry
   sherbet
1 cup heavy cream
1 tablespoon sugar
1 teaspoon vanilla

Boil sugar and water together until sugar has dissolved. Remove from heat and add rum.

Cut sponge cake into three layers. Pour 1/3 of the rum syrup over first layer and cover with vanilla ice cream. Top with second slice; pour 1/3 of rum syrup over that; top with sherbet. Top with last slice, pour remaining rum syrup on top. Put in freezer until finished with the next step.

Whip cream with sugar and vanilla. Remove cake from freezer and frost with whipped cream. Serve immediately, or freeze until about half an hour before serving time.

Serves 12. About 335 calories per serving.

Start to serve time: 15 minutes.

Here again, you can use any combination of ice cream and sherbet or all ice cream if that makes you happy. This keeps, unfrosted, tightly wrapped in the freezer for about a week.

YODEL-LOO

1-1/2 dozen "Yodels"
1 quart vanilla ice cream

Slice Yodels, line bottom of 10-inch spring-form pan. Alternate rest of Yodels and ice cream in pan, ending with Yodels, and freeze until firm.

Serves 12. About 340 calories per serving.
Preparation time: 10 minutes; Freeze time: 2 hours.

ICE CREAM TO TASTE

These ideas give some of the easiest ways to fancy up ice cream I know. The combinations below are just suggestions; you can use any flavor ice cream and almost any complementary flavoring.

Into one pint of slightly softened ice cream, mix any of the following and serve, or freeze until you're ready:

Vanilla Ice Cream

2 tablespoons instant coffee mixed with 1 ounce Irish whiskey

1 10-oz. package frozen strawberries or raspberries

1-1/2 teaspoons almond extract plus 1/4 cup chopped, toasted almonds

1/2 cup mashed bananas plus 1 tablespoon banana liqueur

1/2 cup crushed peanut brittle

Strawberry Ice Cream

1/2 package frozen strawberries

Chocolate or Coffee Ice Cream

1-1/2 tablespoons instant coffee plus 2 tablespoons cognac or brandy

1/2 cup chocolate morsels

Start to serve time: 5 minutes.

REAL ICE CREAM QUICKIES

In case you've never seen, eaten, or made a parfait or a sundae, you're in for surprises. First, they're lip-smacking good. Second, they take only minutes to prepare. Last, the combinations are endless and up to you. I can only suggest.

Parfaits

Parfaits, which are alternating layers of different ice creams, sherbets, fruits, and so on, are traditionally served in tall thin glasses so that you can see before you taste. What a splendid idea!

Layer any two ice cream flavors; top with your favorite sauce.

Layer one ice cream flavor with one sherbet flavor.

Layer vanilla ice cream with your favorite fruit preserves.

Layer orange sherbet with mixed fruits or fruit cocktail.

Work in twos, threes, or any combination thereof. Don't be afraid to experiment; the worst that could happen is that the parfait will taste only good instead of terrific.

Sundaes

Basically, sundaes are made up of ice cream topped with something wonderful, like:

Hot fudge sauce

Crushed pineapple

Peanuts; peanut butter mixed with honey

Orange sections

Berries

Bananas

Cookie crumbs

Maple syrup

Toasted coconut

Marshmallow cream

Anything else you love a lot!

ICE CREAM SANDWICHES

Easy as 1-2-3! Spread any plain, sliced cake with ice cream, top with another slice of cake, and freeze until ready to eat. They're good on the run, or sit down and eat them with a little whipped cream or your favorite sauce.

If you have no cake, don't despair. Spread graham crackers with jam, then with ice cream, and top with another graham cracker spread with jam. Crunchy ice cream sandwiches! If you like, use chocolate-covered graham crackers and skip the jam.

ICE CREAM BALLS

This is truly a no muss, no fuss dessert of great deliciousness. Make ice cream balls with a melon scoop or tablespoon, and roll them in toasted coconut, granola, chopped nuts, cookie crumbs, grated chocolate, or anything else that sounds good to you. Eat right then and there, or put back in the freezer until you need them.

FRUIT
DESSERTS

5

The easiest dessert in the world — and some claim the best — is a beautiful crisp apple, a ripe banana, a juicy peach. All you have to do is eat — no cooking, no chopping, no cleaning up.

But, should you choose, with a minimum of fuss and bother, you can take that piece of fruit and make it even more spectacular. With a little pinch of this, a scant dollop of that, fruit desserts are easy, quick, and decidedly delicious.

Years ago, finding strawberries in the middle of winter was a rare treat, not to mention an outrageously expensive one. Now you're no longer limited to buying fruits in season — anything is available, any time. You can treat yourself to an extra special dessert made with peaches in the middle of February if you like, fresh, if you can afford it, fresh-frozen at most supermarkets, if you can't.

FRUIT BUYING HINTS

With seasonal or out-of-season fruit, check very carefully before you buy; it's pretty perishable, and ripe fruit should be used right away. Here are a few things to look for:

As a general rule, avoid like the plague any fruits that are soft, wrinkled and spotted, bruised, or crushed. With berries in particular, check to see that the bottom of the carton is not stained with juice. If it is, it may contain mashed fruit, topped by a few perfect specimens of berrydom.

If you plan to use bananas right away, buy ones that are yellow from tip to tip, with only a few brown spots. If they are a little green, they'll ripen in a few days at home.

It's hard to judge citrus fruits accurately because some skin bruises do not affect what's inside. As a rule of thumb, if it feels spongy, put it back.

To check ripeness in a melon, don't rely on smell alone. Give a little push with your thumb on the stem end, and if it yields a little, it's ripe and ready. If it's soft all over, it's probably overripe. For watermelons, try to buy large slices or quarters so you can check to see that the color is good and red, the seeds dark, and there are no white streaks running through it.

Don't buy fruit that's too green (unless that's its real color). Peaches should be yellowish, sometimes with a "rosy" blush; nectarines should have an all-over orange-ish color. Buy pears when they're firm and let them ripen at home, out of the sun.

If you can pull a leaf out of the center of the crown of a pineapple, and it gives off a delicious pineapple-y aroma, it's ripe. If it's very dark green in color, it's probably very underripe.

Everybody has a favorite way to ripen fruit at home. Personally, I like to put underripe fruit in a paper bag for a few days, and let it ripen there. Apples, citrus fruits, berries, and bananas you don't have to worry about. If you're buying more than one piece of fruit at a time, try to select pieces of varying degrees of ripeness, so that they won't all be ready to eat — then ready to throw out — at the same time.

COOKING HINTS

To skin fruits such as peaches or apricots, dip them in boiling water for about a minute. The skins will slip right off.

To remove the white membrane from citrus fruit, soak them in boiling water for a few minutes; they'll be easy to peel.

To get the most juice out of a lemon, lime, or orange, roll it on a cutting board or table top, pressing down on it with your hand, before cutting and squeezing it. One medium orange will give you about 1/3 cup of juice; 1 lemon or lime about 2 tablespoons.

Always have grated orange and lemon peel on hand; store them in plastic bags in the freezer. From one orange you'll get about 4 tablespoons of rind; from one lemon or lime, about 2 or 3 teaspoons.

ROSY APPLE RINGS

1 cup sugar
1 cup water
4 apples, cored and
*   sliced into rings*
1/2 teaspoon
*   cinnamon*

Boil sugar and water together for ten minutes, or until it becomes syrupy. Drop apple rings into syrup, add cinnamon, and cook until apples are tender but not mushy, about 8 to 10 minutes.

Serves 4. About 275 calories per serving.
Start to serve time: 20 minutes.

This dessert is a cross between applesauce and baked apples. You can eat it just the way it is, or serve it over ice cream or cake or topped with whipped cream or yogurt.

LAYERED APPLESAUCE PARFAIT

*1/2 cup butter or
  margarine*
2 cups quick oats
2 tablespoons sugar
1 pound applesauce

Melt butter or margarine in skillet; add oats and cook till golden; add sugar and stir. Alternate with applesauce in individual dishes.

Serves 6. About 110 calories per serving.
Start to serve time: 10 minutes.

APRICOTS À LA CRÈME

*1 pound apricots,
  unpeeled*
1/3 cup sugar
*1/2 teaspoon
  cinnamon*
1/4 cup heavy cream

Preheat oven to 375°F.

Halve and pit apricots. Put in one-quart baking dish and cover with sugar, cinnamon, and 1/3 cup water. Bake 20 minutes; pour cream on top and bake 4 minutes longer.

Serves 4. About 172 calories per serving.
Start to serve time: 25-30 minutes.

To use canned apricots, just heat them in the oven in their own syrup, to which you've added cinnamon, for about 10 minutes; then add cream. Try it with pears or peaches.

APRICOTS JULEP

8 apricot halves
*8 tablespoons mint
  jelly*
2 drops mint extract

Heat jelly with extract; pour over apricots in saucepan. Heat through for 5 minutes.

Serves 8. About 90 calories per serving.
Start to serve time: 10 minutes.

Again, you may substitute any fruit you like — peaches, pears, pineapple slices.

BANANA POPSICLES

4 semi-ripe bananas
chocolate syrup
chopped nuts
coconut

Peel bananas, cut in half crosswise. Put a wooden skewer, plastic fork or popsicle stick in cut end of each half. Roll in any of three toppings, or any combination. Wrap loosely in aluminum foil or freezer paper and freeze till firm.

Serves 8. About 150 calories each.
Preparation time: 5 minutes; Freeze time: 2 hours.

CRUNCHY BANANAS

2 large bananas
2 tablespoons sifted
  cornstarch
2 tablespoons butter
1 cup sugar
1/3 cup water
1/4 cup sesame seeds
Ice water

Peel bananas; cut into 2-inch slices. Dip them lightly into cornstarch, and lightly brown in melted butter.

Combine sugar and water; let cook until thick and syrupy. Add sesame seeds.

To Serve: Bring the bananas, the syrup, and the ice water to the table. Be sure the water is *very* cold (float some ice cubes in it) and the syrup *very* hot (let it bubble). Dip the bananas into the syrup, coating thickly, then immediately into the ice water. If everything turns out right, the syrup will immediately harden and you will have crunchy bananas. If it doesn't quite harden, don't worry. It will still taste delicious.

Serves 4. About 340 calories per serving.
Start to serve time: 15-20 minutes.

You can make the same dessert with peeled apple wedges.

FRIED BANANAS

2 bananas
1 egg
3 tablespoons rum
1/4 cup butter or oil
1/4 cup bread crumbs

Peel bananas; cut into 2-inch pieces. Soak in rum. Heat butter or oil in skillet over high heat. Beat egg; dip bananas in egg, then bread crumbs; fry until golden brown.

Serves 4. About 245 calories per serving.

Start to serve time: 10 minutes.

BLACKBERRY "STEW"

2 cups blackberries
2 cups water
1 cup sugar
4 tablespoons
   cornstarch
1/4 teaspoon salt
1 tablespoon lemon
   juice

Cook berries in water until soft. Mix together sugar, cornstarch, and salt; add slowly to berries, stirring constantly. Bring to a boil; cook 5 minutes. Remove from heat and add lemon juice. Serve hot with sugar and cream.

Serves 4. About 265 calories per serving.

Start to serve time: 15 minutes.

CANTALOUPE LIME RICKEY

cantaloupe balls
1/2 cup sugar
1/2 cup water
2 drops mint extract
3 tablespoons chopped
   mint
juice of 2 limes

Boil sugar and water until syrupy, about 10 minutes. Add extract and chopped mint. Cool and add lime juice; pour over cantaloupe and chill about 1 hour.

Serves 4. About 130 calories per serving.

Preparation time: 15 minutes; Chill time: 1/2 hour or more.

CANTALOUPE SOUP

1 cantaloupe (about 3
   pounds)
1/2 cup dry sherry
1/4 cup sugar
*1 tablespoon lime
   juice*

Remove rind and seeds from cantaloupe; cut into chunks. Put melon and rest of ingredients in blender and blend on high speed until smooth. Chill thoroughly before serving.

Serves 5. About 110 calories per serving.

Preparation time: 10 minutes; Chill time: 1/2 hour or more.

PORT SALUTE

*1 small cantaloupe or
   honeydew*
2 tablespoons sugar
3/4 cup port

Halve melon, remove seeds. Sprinkle each half with 1 tablespoon sugar and put half of port in each half melon. Chill.

Serves 4–6. About 120 calories per serving.

Preparation time: 5 minutes; Chill time: 1/2 hour or more.

Try this with pear halves or peach halves — terrific!

FROZEN MELON TREATS

Watermelon
Cantaloupe
Honeydew
Confectioners sugar

Cut melon into pieces about 2 inches by 4 inches. Put popsicle stick or plastic knife into one end, and roll fruit in confectioners sugar. Freeze until firm.

Preparation time: 5 minutes; Freeze time: 1-1/2 to 2 hours.

MINTED GRAPES

1 bunch seedless green
   grapes
1/2 cup honey
2 tablespoons lime
   juice
2 tablespoons finely
   chopped fresh mint,
   or half the amount
   dried

Wash and dry grapes; remove from stem. Place in serving bowl. Combine rest of ingredients; pour over grapes and refrigerate.

Serves 4. About 153 calories per serving.
Preparation time: 5 minutes; Chill time: 1/2 hour or more.

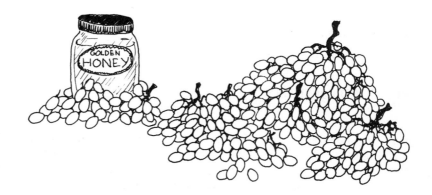

HOT FRUIT DESSERT

3 small cans mandarin
   oranges
3 small cans pineapple
   chunks
3 small cans pears
3 #2 cans pitted Bing
   cherries
3 lemons
1-1/2 cups brown
   sugar

Drain fruit. Grate lemon rind into sugar; slice lemons very thin. Layer fruits, including lemons, in baking dish, sprinkling sugar mixture in between each one. Heat in oven until very hot. Serve with whipped or sour cream.

Serves 8. About 200 calories per serving.
Start to serve time: 20 minutes.

ORANGES À L'ORANGE

4 large navel oranges
1/4 cup confectioners
 sugar
8 tablespoons
 Cointreau or other
 orange liqueur
3/4 cup heavy cream
2 tablespoons
 superfine sugar
grated rind of 2
 lemons
juice of 1 lemon

Peel oranges, making sure to remove all membranes. Section, put in bowl, and sprinkle with confectioners sugar. Add 6 tablespoons liqueur and lemon juice; refrigerate.

Whip cream with superfine sugar and remaining liqueur. Spoon over oranges.

Serves 6. About 207 calories per serving.

Preparation time: 20 minutes; Chill time: 1/2 hour or more.

POACHED ORANGES

rind of 6 navel
 oranges
2 cups sugar
3 oranges, peeled and
 sectioned
2 tablespoons orange
 liqueur

Chop orange rind, mix with sugar and 1 cup water. Cook over medium heat until thick, about 10 minutes. Add orange segments and cook over low heat, basting, for 5 minutes. Remove from heat; add liqueur; chill.

Serves 4. About 455 calories per serving.

Preparation time: 15 minutes; Chill time: 1/2 hour or more.

PEACHES IN CUSTARD

12 peach halves
1 cup sugar
6 egg yolks
3/4 cup fresh orange
 juice
3/4 cup dry sherry
1 cup heavy cream,
 whipped

Chill peach halves. In top of double boiler, combine sugar and yolks and beat until thick and lemon-colored. Add juice and sherry and place over simmering water. Stir until thick and custardy. Chill. Just before serving, fold custard into whipped cream and serve over peaches.

Serves 6-12. About 208 calories per serving.

Preparation time: 15 minutes; Chill time: About 1/2 hour.

GINGER PEACHY

2 cups sugar
1 cup water
1 teaspoon candied
  ginger, chopped
1 tablespoon lemon
  juice
2 teaspoons grated
  lemon rind
12 peach halves
1/2 cup sherry
1/2 cup brandy

Bring sugar, water, ginger, lemon juice, and rind to a boil; let simmer 5 minutes. Place peach halves, hollow side down, in syrup. Cover and poach 10 minutes. Remove to serving dish. Add sherry and brandy to syrup; boil 3 minutes. Pour over peaches and chill.

Serves 6. About 300 calories per serving.

Preparation time: 20 minutes; Chill time: 1/2 hour or more.

PEACH MERINGUE

2 peach halves
1 tablespoon jam
1 egg white
2 tablespoons sugar

Place peach halves in pan; place half a tablespoon jam in center of each.

Beat egg white until stiff, at high speed; add sugar gradually till dissolved. Cover each peach half completely. Broil 1 or 2 minutes until golden brown.

Serves 1 or 2. About 125 calories per peach half.

Start to serve time: 10 minutes.

PEACHES 'N CREAM

*1 8-oz. package
cream cheese,
softened
2 tablespoons lemon
juice
2/3 cup heavy cream
Sliced peaches, fresh,
canned, or frozen*

Beat cream cheese with lemon juice until fluffy; gradually beat in heavy cream. Chill until ready to serve. Spoon over peaches.

Serves 8. About 220 calories per serving.

Preparation time: 5 minutes; Chill time: 1/2 hour or more.

This is particularly terrific over fresh peaches, but not too bad over strawberries, either.

PEACHES OLÉ

*1 16-oz. can peach
halves
3 tablespoons brown
sugar
2 tablespoons lime
juice
1/4 cup sherry
1 tablespoon grated
lime peel*

Drain peaches, reserving 1/2 cup liquid. Combine syrup, brown sugar, lime juice, and sherry in saucepan; heat through, about 5 minutes. Put peach halves flat side down in serving dish; pour syrup over; sprinkle with lime peel. Chill until ready to serve.

Serves 8. About 132 calories per serving.

Preparation time: 5 minutes; Chill time: 1/2 hour or more.

For a slightly different accent, try substituting apricot preserves for lime juice, and grated orange peel for lime peel.

PEARS FRANÇAISE

*1 8-oz. can pear halves
1/2 cup strawberries
2 tablespoons sugar
slivered toasted
almonds
whipped cream*

Drain pear halves and chill. Put strawberries and sugar in blender, blend until smooth. Pour over pears, sprinkle with almonds. Serve with whipped cream, if desired.

Serves 2. About 240 calories per serving.

Start to serve time: 10 minutes.

BUTTERED PINEAPPLE SPEARS

1/4 fresh pineapple
1/4 cup butter

Slice pineapple into spears. Heat butter and brown pineapple quickly over high heat.

Serves 2. About 230 calories per serving.

Start to serve time: 5 minutes.

POACHED PLUMS

1 pound Italian plums
1/2 cup sugar
1-1/2 cups water
2 slices lemon

Halve plums, remove pits. Combine sugar and water and boil about 6 minutes. Add plums and lemon. Bring to a boil and then reduce heat to simmer; cook about 4 minutes. Cool; refrigerate until chilled.

Serves 6. About 115 calories per serving.

Preparation time: 15 minutes; Chill time: 1/2 hour or more.

RASPBERRIES ON CREAM

whipped cream
sugar
vanilla
raspberries
powdered sugar

Whip cream with sugar and vanilla until stiff. Mound on serving dish and put chilled raspberries in center. Sprinkle with powdered sugar.

Start to serve time: 10 minutes.

STRAWBERRIES ÉLÉGANT

*1-1/2 cups sliced
   strawberries
1/4 cup brown sugar
1/2 cup sour cream*

Sprinkle most of brown sugar over strawberries, reserving about 1 teaspoon. Top with sour cream and sprinkle reserved sugar over all.

Serves 4. About 145 calories per serving.
Start to serve time: 3 minutes.

To make "Anything Élégant," just substitute seedless white grapes for the strawberries, or fresh peaches, nectarines, bananas, or blueberries.

STRAWBERRIES IN KIRSCH

*2 pounds strawberries
powdered sugar
1/2 cup Kirsch
whipped cream*

Wash and hull strawberries; sprinkle with powdered sugar and Kirsch. Top with whipped cream.

Serves 4. About 235 calories per serving.
Start to serve time: 5 minutes.

STRAWBERRIES MELBA

*1 quart fresh
   strawberries
1 10-oz. package
   frozen raspberries
1/4 cup crème de cassis
1/2 teaspoon lemon
   juice
pinch of salt*

Wash and hull strawberries. Sprinkle lightly with sugar. Purée raspberries in blender; strain to remove seeds, if desired. Stir cassis, lemon juice, and salt into purée; chill well. Serve over strawberries.

Serves 4. About 135 calories per serving.
Preparation time: 10 minutes; Chill time: 1/2 hour or more.

If you don't happen to have crème de cassis, you can use Kirsch, Grand Marnier, or Curacao, rum, or a dry white wine.

STRAWBERRIES PARISIENNE

1 quart strawberries
1 10-oz. package
  frozen raspberries
1 tablespoon Kirsch
1/4 cup confectioners
  sugar
1/2 cup heavy cream,
  whipped

Wash and hull strawberries, put in serving bowl. Purée raspberries in blender with Kirsch and sugar to taste. Strain and pour over strawberries. Chill several hours. Serve with whipped cream.

Serves 4. About 285 calories per serving.

Preparation time: 10 minutes; Chill time: at least 2 hours.

TORCHY TOUCHES

Nothing is more impressive to a tableful of dinner guests than a flaming dessert — which, in actuality, took you only about three minutes to do. The trick to successful flambéeing is to heat the brandy just before applying the match.

The basic recipe is the same for all the fruits mentioned here; the ingredients vary only slightly. Any combination of fruit and liqueur is good. Serve them as is or over ice cream or plain cake.

Cherries

1 16-oz. can pitted
  black cherries,
  drained
2 oz. Cointreau
2 oz. warm brandy

Pour Cointreau over cherries and let stand. Just before serving, heat brandy, pour over cherries, and ignite.

Serves 6–8. About 114 calories per serving.

Peaches

6 to 8 fresh ripe
 peaches or 2 10-oz.
 packages frozen,
 defrosted
4 oz. peach or apricot
 brandy
2 oz. warm brandy

If using fresh peaches, peel and slice; if frozen, drain. Pour apricot or peach brandy over them; let stand until ready to serve. Add heated brandy and ignite.

Serves 6–8. About 114 calories per serving.

Strawberries

2 pints fresh
 strawberries or 2
 10-oz. packages
 frozen, defrosted
1/2 cup sugar
2 oz. warm brandy

Wash and hull fresh berries; drain frozen. Sprinkle with sugar and let stand. Pour warm brandy over; ignite.

Serves 6–8. About 171 calories per serving.

BANANAS FLAMBÉE

2 bananas
2 tablespoons butter
1 teaspoon
  cinnamon
2 tablespoons brown
  sugar
3 tablespoons warm
  brandy or rum; or 2
  tablespoons brandy
  or rum, 1
  tablespoon banana
  liqueur

Peel bananas; slice in half lengthwise and crosswise. Melt butter; add bananas, cut side up. Cook until browned, turn, sprinkle with cinnamon and sugar, and cook until sugar has dissolved. Pour warm brandy or rum over bananas and ignite.

Serves 4. About 65 calories per serving.

Start to serve time: 7 minutes.

PEACHES AND CHERRIES FLAMBÉE

3/4 cup currant jelly
1 cup peach halves
2 cups pitted dark
  cherries
1/2 cup brandy

Melt jelly; drain fruit and heat in jelly. Pour brandy over all and heat through; ignite.

Serves 8. About 315 calories per serving.

Start to serve time: 10 minutes.

PARTY PINEAPPLE

1 pineapple
1/4 cup sugar
1/2 cup water
1/2 cup sherry
1-1/2 cups currant
  jelly
1/2 cup cognac

Peel pineapple and cut into thin slices. Combine sugar, water, and sherry, and bring to a boil. Add pineapple slices and cook about 5 minutes. Drain. Melt jelly over low heat, add pineapple, and simmer 5 minutes. Add cognac and heat through. Ignite cognac and spoon flaming syrup over fruit.

Serves 6. About 260 calories per serving.

Start to serve time: 10 minutes.

PLUMS À LA RUSSE

1 lb. plums, fresh or
  canned
1/4 cup water
1/2 cup sugar
1/4 teaspoon
  cinnamon
1/2 teaspoon almond
  extract
1/2 teaspoon vanilla
  extract
1 tablespoon vodka

Halve plums, remove pits. Boil water, sugar, and cinnamon in a small saucepan for 10 minutes, until sugar is dissolved. Add plums and cook about 8 minutes, until tender but still firm. Remove and cool to room temperature. Put extracts and vodka into small saucepan. Heat nearly to boiling. Ignite with a match and pour over plums.

Serves 4. About 188 calories per serving.

Start to serve time: About 1/2 hour.

FRUIT AND CHEESE

Gourmets all over the world have always considered fruit and cheese to be the perfect ending to a meal. Why shouldn't you? It's easy. It's certainly fast. It's low in calories (an ounce of cheese is between 85 and 105 calories), nutritious (cheese is a terrific source of protein; fruits supply the vitamins), and whatever combination tastes good to you, is good. Here are a few combinations I like, but anything goes, so be inventive:

Sharp cheddar with apples, pears
Port du Salut with fresh figs, plums
Gruyere or Swiss with bananas, apples
Brie or Camembert with oranges, pineapple
Gouda or Edam with grapes, melon, apricots
Fontina or Bel Paese with cherries, raisins

CAKES, PIES, AND COOKIES

6

Bet you never thought a whipped-cream-topped strawberry rum cake would take only 15 minutes — start to finish — to prepare. It can and does (see page 77). Most of the other recipes in this chapter take as little time. They start with store-bought cakes, and you take it from there (except for a few that are easy and fast to do from scratch). By the time you're finished fancying them up, no one will realize you haven't baked them yourself.

I always keep a frozen pound cake and a couple of frozen pie crusts around for emergencies. They've saved many an unexpected dinner from being dessertless. Cookies have a wonderful way of becoming delicious bottoms for scrumptious toppings or surprising desserts themselves when filled, stacked, and sliced into, for example, a Quick, Quick Cake (see page 75).

As any dessert based on cake or pie immediately adds calories, be sure to plan around that if you're counting. If you're eating alone, use just one slice of cake (where the recipe calls for a whole cake) and proportionately less of the other ingredients. Then you won't be tempted to eat more than you should and won't have leftovers for indiscriminate nibbling.

COOKING HINTS

If you are going to pre-bake a frozen pie crust, prick it all over with a fork first, so that it will bake evenly and not bubble up.

Don't throw away stale cake. Break it up into small pieces and throw it in the blender; cake crumbs make excellent toppings for desserts.

Cottage cheese whips up really nicely in the blender; add a little milk and blend at high speed until smooth. Sweetened and flavored, it makes a delicious "cheesecake" in a pre-made crust.

You can slice, individually wrap, and then freeze plain cake. Use the slices as you need to without having to buy or defrost a whole one, just for yourself.

Check your local supermarket for "day-old" sponge, pound, or angel food cakes. If you're going to use them as the base for a tasty filling or flavorful topping, they're perfectly fine, and often much cheaper.

APPLE "CAKE"

9 slices of thin-sliced
  white bread
1/3 cup butter or
  margarine,
  softened
1/2 cup strawberry
  jam
2 apples
1/4 cup sifted flour
1/4 cup brown sugar,
  firmly packed
1/4 teaspoon
  cinnamon
2 tablespoons butter
  or margarine

Preheat oven to 425° F.

Trim crust from bread. Spread each slice with butter and jam. Make three stacks of three, and place close together on a baking sheet. Peel and slice apples very thin; arrange on top of stacks. Combine sugar, flour, cinnamon, and butter until crumbly; sprinkle over tops of stacks.

Bake at 425° F. for 10 minutes.

Serves 3–4. About 200 calories per serving.
Start to serve time: 20-25 minutes.

APRICOT ANGEL CAKE

1 large jar baby-food
  apricot purée
2 teaspoons lemon
  juice
5 teaspoons butter or
  margarine
2 tablespoons
  cornstarch
1/2 cup (or more)
  apricot juice or
  water
1 10-inch angel food
  cake

Mix purée and lemon juice; set aside. Melt butter in a skillet, add cornstarch, stirring until well mixed. Add juice or water and cook, stirring, until thickened. Remove from heat and add purée to the sauce. Spread on top of cake and let drip down the sides.

Serves 12. About 225 calories per slice.
Start to serve time: 14 minutes.

Good with pears or peaches, too.

BLUEBERRY SLUMP

2 cups blueberries
1/2 cup sugar
1 cup water
1 cup flour
2 teaspoons baking
* powder*
1/4 teaspoon salt
2 tablespoons butter
1/3 cup milk

Preheat oven to 400° F.

Cook blueberries, sugar, and water over low heat in an oven-proof pan until sugar has dissolved. Raise heat to medium.

Mix remaining ingredients together, and drop by tablespoons on top of blueberries. Bake 20 minutes in 400° F. oven, till browned.

Serves 6. About 210 calories per serving.

Start to serve time: 1/2 hour.

BLUEBERRY TOAST CAKE

3 cups blueberries
3/4 cup sugar
pinch salt
1/2 teaspoon lemon
* juice*
dash of cinnamon
4 slices French toast

Preheat oven to 425° F.

Cook blueberries with sugar, salt, and lemon juice for 10 minutes. Pour into shallow baking dish; top with French toast slices. Sprinkle with cinnamon, and a little confectioners sugar, if desired. Bake at 425° F. for 20 minutes.

Serves 4. 138 calories per serving.

Start to serve time: 30 minutes.

DAY-AHEAD CHEESECAKE

2 8-oz. packages
  cream cheese,
  softened
1 cup sugar
3 eggs
1 pint sour cream
1 teaspoon vanilla

Preheat oven to 325°F.

Put cream cheese in blender, a little at a time, and blend until smooth. Add sugar; blend again. Add eggs, one at a time, blending after each addition. Add sour cream and vanilla, and blend until smooth.

Pour mixture into a 9- or 10-inch spring form pan greased and sprinkled with graham cracker or cookie crumbs.

Bake for 1/2 hour. Turn oven off, but leave cake in oven 1 hour with door closed. Chill overnight.

Serves 8. About 375 calories per serving.
Preparation time: 6 minutes; Chill time: Overnight.

I included this recipe for two reasons, despite the fact that it has to chill overnight to be at its best. First, it is truly easy to prepare. Second, it is one of the lightest, yet richest and most delicious cheesecakes you'll ever taste. Plan ahead for this one; it's well worth the trouble.

CLAFOUTI

3-1/2 tablespoons
  butter
3 cups strawberries,
  sliced apples, pears,
  or any other fruit
4 eggs
1 cup milk
1/4 cup cream
pinch salt
1/4 teaspoon nutmeg
1 teaspoon lemon
  juice
1 tablespoon vanilla
2 tablespoons orange
  liqueur
1-1/4 cups flour
1/2 cup sugar

Preheat oven to 350°F.

Melt butter; use 1/2 tablespoon to grease an 8-inch pie pan. Combine the remaining butter with all ingredients except flour and sugar in a blender; blend until smooth. Add flour and sugar, blend until well combined. Spread fruit in bottom of pan; pour batter over. Bake at 350°F. for 30 minutes or until browned.

Serves 8. About 275 calories per serving.
Start to serve time: 45 minutes, but worth it.

EASY CINNAMON/ORANGE DANISH

1 8-oz. package
refrigerator
buttermilk rolls
butter or margarine
1/4 cup orange
marmalade
2 tablespoons sugar
1 teaspoon cinnamon
1/4 cup finely
chopped walnuts

Preheat oven to 400° F. Lightly grease a cookie sheet.

Flatten each roll to a four-inch circle; spread with butter or margarine and marmalade. Combine sugar, cinnamon, and nuts; sprinkle a little over each roll. Cut each one in half, and place one half on top of the other. Pinch ends together with a little twist and place on cookie sheet. Bake about 10 minutes, or until golden.

Makes 10. About 150 calories each.
Start to serve time: 15 minutes.

COFFEE/CREAM CAKE

3 dozen ladyfingers
3 cups heavy cream
3 teaspoons instant
coffee
3 tablespoons cocoa
2 tablespoons sugar

Split ladyfingers and line the bottom and sides of a 9-inch spring form pan. Whip the cream, adding instant coffee, cocoa, and sugar gradually. Spread one third of mixture over ladyfingers; top with another layer of ladyfingers. Repeat, ending with whipped cream. Chill until firm enough to remove the sides of the pan.

Serves 12. 380 calories per serving.
Preparation time: 14 minutes; Chill time: 2 hours or more.

EASY RUM CAKE

*1 frozen or packaged
  pound cake, sliced*
1 cup sugar
1/2 cup water
1/2 cup dark rum
1 cup heavy cream
2 tablespoons sugar

Place slices of cake on individual dishes; set aside. Boil sugar and water until it forms a thread when dropped into a glass of cold water (about 5 or 6 minutes). Cool slightly and add the rum.

Whip cream with sugar. Slowly dribble rum sauce over each slice of cake; using only as much as can be absorbed. Top with whipped cream.

Serves 12. 285 calories per slice.

Start to serve time: 15 minutes.

FRENCH-TOASTED FRUIT CAKE

2 slices pound cake
2 tablespoons butter
2 tablespoons jam
any fresh fruit, sliced
*1/2 cup heavy cream,
  whipped*

Spread cake slices with butter and fry until golden. Spread one side of each slice with jam; top with fruit, and top it all off with whipped cream.

Serves 2. About 100 calories per slice.

Start to serve time: 6 minutes.

FRUIT CAKE

1 package refrigerator
  crescent rolls
1/2 cup cookie
  crumbs
1 tablespoon sugar
1 teaspoon cinnamon
dash of nutmeg
2 cups mixed fresh,
  frozen, or canned
  fruit, well drained
3 tablespoons melted
  butter or margarine

Preheat oven to 375° F.

Unroll crescent rolls and press into a greased rectangular baking pan. Combine cookie crumbs, sugar, cinnamon, and nutmeg; sprinkle over rolls. Spread fruit on top; brush with melted butter or margarine. Bake 30 minutes, or until golden.

Serves 8. 245 calories per serving.

Start to serve time: 40 minutes.

This takes a little longer than most of the other recipes, but it's worth it.

INSTANT PUDDING CAKE

1/2 cup heavy cream,
  whipped
1 package instant
  pudding, lemon,
  vanilla, or
  butterscotch,
  prepared according
  to directions but
  using only 1 cup
  milk
12 ladyfingers
1/4 cup confectioners
  sugar, sifted
2 tablespoons
  semi-sweet
  chocolate morsels,
  melted

Fold prepared pudding into whipped cream. Place four ladyfingers on a plate; spread with two thirds of the pudding; repeat, ending with ladyfingers. Mix confectioners sugar with a little water until smooth; dribble over ladyfingers. Pour melted chocolate over all in zig-zag design. Serve right away or chill until ready.

Serves 6. About 120 calories per serving.

Start to serve time: 15 minutes.

This looked so beautiful when done, it almost wasn't served —but everyone was delighted when it tasted as good as it looked.

ITALIAN-STYLE REFRIGERATOR CAKE

1 pound cake
1 lb. ricotta cheese
1/2 cup sugar
2 oz. semi-sweet
chocolate morsels
1 cup raw apple,
grated
1 teaspoon almond
extract
1 cup heavy cream,
whipped
1/2 cup chopped nuts

Slice pound cake thinly. Mix ricotta with sugar, chocolate morsels, apple, and almond extract. Spread between cake slices, and reassemble as a loaf. Chill until ready to serve, or fold nuts into whipped cream, spread over cake, and serve immediately.

Serves 12. 370 calories per serving.

Start to serve time: 15 minutes.

"JELLY ROLLS" THE EASY WAY

12 slices white bread
1/4 cup brown sugar,
packed
1/4 cup softened
butter or margarine
3/4 cup grated
coconut
6 tablespoons
strawberry jam
6 tablespoons
peanut butter

Preheat oven to 425° F.

Remove crusts from bread and roll each slice with a rolling pin until flattened out. Mix butter or margarine with sugar, and spread evenly on all slices of bread. Dip buttered side into coconut; spread about 1/2 tablespoon peanut butter and 1/2 tablespoon jelly on plain side. Roll each one up like a jelly roll and place, seam side down, on cookie sheet. Bake 4 to 5 minutes, until golden.

Makes 12. About 235 calories per roll.

Start to serve time: 15 minutes.

MOCK FRUIT CAKE

*1 9- or 10-inch layer
    cake, yellow or
    white
1/3 cup jelly
1 30-oz. can pear
    halves, drained
1 8-oz. can
    pineapple chunks,
    drained
2 tablespoons brown
    sugar
dash of cinnamon
2 tablespoons butter
    or margarine*

Spread the cake with jelly; top with fruits. Mix brown sugar, cinnamon, and butter together, dot over cake. Broil about 3 or 4 minutes.

Serves 8. About 180 calories per serving.
Start to serve time: About 6 minutes.

NO-BAKE CAKE

*12 graham cracker
    squares
1 cup butter or
    margarine, softened
4 cups sugar
3 tablespoons cocoa
3 eggs
1/4 cup orange juice*

Cream butter or margarine with sugar until fluffy. Add cocoa and eggs, mixing well. Add enough orange juice so mixture becomes spreadable, but not runny.

Arrange a layer of graham crackers on the bottom of a wax-paper lined square cake pan. Cover with chocolate mixture. Repeat until chocolate mixture is used up, ending with graham crackers. Let set in the refrigerator about an hour. Serve in slices.

Serves 8. About 500 calories per slice.
Preparation time: 10 minutes; Chill time: 1 hour.

ONE-PAN CHOCOLATE CAKE

1-1/2 cups flour
1/2 cup cocoa
1 cup sugar
1 teaspoon baking
soda
1/2 teaspoon salt
1 cup cold water
1/2 cup oil
2 teaspoons vanilla
2 tablespoons vinegar

Preheat oven to 350° F.

Measure all ingredients into an 8-inch square pan or 9-inch round pan EXCEPT VINEGAR. Stir well until thoroughly blended. Add vinegar; stir quickly and thoroughly and place immediately in preheated 350° F. oven.

THERE MUST BE NO DELAY IN BAKING AFTER ADD-ING VINEGAR.

Bake for 20 to 25 minutes, or until center springs back and sides pull away from pan.

Serves 8. About 210 calories per serving.
Start to serve time: 1/2 hour.

PEACHY POUND CAKE

1 frozen pound cake,
thawed
3 cups peach yogurt
2 tablespoons peach
brandy (optional)
canned or fresh
peaches, sliced

Mix yogurt and brandy together. Slice pound cake into three layers; spread yogurt mixture in between. Wrap in aluminum foil until ready to serve. Slice thinly and top with peach slices to serve.

Serves 12. About 172 calories per slice.
Start to serve time: 10 minutes.

This works equally well with any fruit-flavored yogurt and fruit, or coffee- or vanilla-flavored yogurt mixed with brandy, cognac, or rum.

PEAR CRISP

3 cups sliced pears
4 tablespoons lemon
    juice
2 tablespoons sherry
dash of cinnamon
1/3 cup flour
1 cup quick-cooking
    oats
1/2 cup brown sugar,
    firmly packed
1/3 cup melted butter
    or margarine

Preheat oven to 350° F.

Put pears in the bottom of a greased baking dish; sprinkle with lemon juice, sherry, and cinnamon.

Combine flour, oats, brown sugar, and melted butter or margarine; mix until well blended. Sprinkle over pears and bake for about 20 minutes, or until golden brown.

Serves 8. About 200 calories per serving.

Start to serve time: 1/2 hour.

POUND CAKE SUPREME

1 pound cake
4 tablespoons sherry
1 12-oz. jar apricot or
    pineapple preserves
1 16.5-oz. can
    chocolate frosting

Cut pound cake into 4 layers. Spread two layers with preserves; 1 layer with chocolate frosting; stack, alternating layers. Frost with remaining frosting.

Serves 10–12. About 485 calories per slice.

Start to serve time: 15 minutes.

POUND CAKE SURPRISE

1/2 cup confectioners
    sugar, sifted
1 tablespoon grated
    lemon rind
3 teaspoons lemon
    juice
1 pound cake

Blend confectioners sugar, lemon rind, and lemon juice until smooth and spreadable. Spread over pound cake.

Serves 10. About 170 calories per serving.

Start to serve time: 4 minutes.

If you really want to be fancy, decorate the top of the glazed cake with lemon slices. For a different version, substitute orange rind and orange juice.

QUICK CAKE ÉLÉGANT

4 slices angel food
  cake
4 tablespoons butter
  or margarine,
  softened
2 tablespoons brown
  sugar

Spread each slice of cake with butter or margarine and sprinkle with brown sugar. Broil about 2 minutes or until glazed.

Serves 4. About 200 calories per serving.

Start to serve time: 4 minutes.

Couldn't be any quicker, but could be a little different if you added some grated coconut or chopped nuts.

QUICK COBBLER

1 large can pear halves,
  drained
1 tablespoon lemon
  juice
1/3 cup brown sugar,
  firmly packed
3 tablespoons melted
  butter or margarine
1 package refrigerator
  cinnamon rolls

Preheat oven to 375° F.

Place pear halves in baking pan; sprinkle with lemon juice, brown sugar, and butter or margarine. Heat in the oven until sugar is melted and pears are hot. Top with the cinnamon rolls, reserving icing that comes in the package. Bake about 20 minutes or until golden. Ice.

Serves 8. About 225 calories per serving.

Start to serve time: 1/2 hour.

QUICK QUICK CAKE

1 8-1/2-oz. package
  chocolate wafers
2 cups heavy cream
1 tablespoon sugar
1 teaspoon vanilla
2 tablespoons cognac
  or chocolate-flavored
  liqueur
grated chocolate

Whip cream with sugar, vanilla, and cognac or liqueur. Using entire package of wafers, spread and stack with whipped cream. Place on its side, like a log, and frost entire roll, top and sides, with whipped cream. Sprinkle with a little grated chocolate and cover loosely with aluminum foil. Freeze at least 15 minutes before serving.

Serves 8. About 252 calories per serving.

Preparation time: 15 minutes; Freeze time: 15 minutes.

ROSY-RED ANGEL CAKE

1 10-inch angel food
  cake
2 10-oz. packages
  frozen raspberries,
  thawed
1-1/2 teaspoons
  lemon juice
1-1/2 teaspoons
  cornstarch mixed
  with 1-1/2
  teaspoons cold
  water
1 peach, sliced

Put cake on serving dish and set aside. Combine all ingredients except the peach in a saucepan and bring to a boil, mashing raspberries as they cook. Stir constantly until mixture is thick.

Arrange peach slices over top of cake. Pour raspberry mixture over all, letting it drip down the sides.

Serves 12. About 165 calories per serving.

Start to serve time: 15 minutes.

SHERRY TRIFLE

24 ladyfingers
1/2 cup cream sherry
1/4 cup strawberry
  jam
2 cups heavy cream,
  whipped

Line a serving dish with ladyfingers, pour sherry over them. Spread strawberry jam over all and top with whipped cream. Chill.

Serves 8. About 400 calories per serving.

Start to serve time: 10 minutes; Chill time: 1/2 hour.

STRAWBERRY CAKE

2 10-inch sponge cake
  layers
1 cup strawberry
  preserves
1 cup pineapple
  preserves
1 cup black raspberry
  preserves
2 cups heavy cream
1/4 cup confectioners
  sugar
2 teaspoons vanilla
fresh strawberries

Cut each layer in half, crosswise. Spread bottom layer with strawberry preserves; top with second layer and spread with pineapple preserves; top with third layer and spread with raspberry preserves; top with fourth layer.

Whip cream with sugar and vanilla until stiff; spread on top and sides of cake. Decorate with whole strawberries.

Serves 12. About 690 calories per serving.

Start to serve time: 18 minutes.

Not only is this very delicious, it's very calorific, too. But save it for a special occasion. By the way, any combination of preserves will work — cherry, apricot, blackberry, blueberry, or even orange marmalade.

STRAWBERRY RUM CAKE

*3 tablespoons butter
   or margarine
3 tablespoons orange
   juice
1/3 cup sugar
1/3 cup rum
2 9- or 10-inch yellow
   or sponge cake
   layers
1 cup heavy cream,
   whipped
fresh strawberries,
   sliced*

Bring butter, orange juice, and sugar to a boil; let cook until syrupy. Remove from heat and stir in rum. Poke holes in both cake layers with a toothpick; pour syrup evenly over each one. Let stand until ready to serve.

When ready, spread half the whipped cream over one layer of cake; top with sliced strawberries. Top with the second layer and cover with remaining whipped cream. Garnish with remaining strawberries.

Serves 12. About 185 calories per slice.

Start to serve time: 15 minutes.

TIPSY ANGEL CAKE

*1 angel food cake
1/4 cup coffee liqueur
3 tablespoons heavy
   cream*

Poke holes along the top of the cake with a shish-kabob skewer or long-tined fork. Mix liqueur and cream together; pour over cake. Let stand about an hour to absorb.

Serves 12. About 180 calories per slice.

Start to serve time: 5 minutes; Stand time: 1 hour.

This will also work well with pound or sponge cake. If you don't have coffee liqueur, mix 1 or 2 teaspoons of instant coffee into brandy or cognac, add a little sugar, and stir until dissolved.

TRIFLING EASY TRIFLE

1 3-1/4-oz. package
  chocolate pudding
  mix
2 cups skim milk
2 10-inch sponge cake
  layers
1 large can pitted dark
  cherries
1 cup heavy cream,
  whipped
1 cup chopped
  walnuts or slivered
  toasted almonds

Prepare chocolate pudding according to directions, using two cups skim rather than whole milk. Cut up the sponge cake into 16 pieces, and put half in the bottom of a large serving bowl. Spread half the chocolate pudding on top of the cake, and half the cherries over that. Repeat. Chill until firm.

Just before serving, whip cream and spoon over trifle. Sprinkle with nuts.

Serves 12. About 170 calories per serving.

Preparation time: 20 minutes; Chill time: 1-2 hours.

VERY CHERRY CRESCENT TWIRLS

1 16-oz. can red
  cherries, pitted
4 tablespoons flour
1 8-oz. can
  refrigerator crescent
  rolls
butter or margarine,
  softened

Preheat oven to 375°F.

Drain cherries thoroughly. Toss with flour to coat. Unroll the rolls, but do not separate; spread with softened butter or margarine. Spread cherries onto the dough and roll up as you would a jelly roll. Cut each piece into three slices, and bake, cut side down, on a cookie sheet, for about 20 minutes.

Serves 6. About 230 calories per serving.

Start to serve time: 1/2 hour.

ZUPPA INGLESE PRESTO

1 sponge cake
rum
crème de cacao
1 cup heavy cream,
* whipped with a*
* little sugar*
shaved or grated
* chocolate*

Cut the sponge cake into serving slices, about a half-inch thick. Sprinkle rum over half the slices; crème de cacao over the rest. Cover half the slices with whipped cream, and place the remaining slices on top. If you use both rum and crème de cacao, alternate slices. Cover with more whipped cream and sprinkle with chocolate.

Serves 12. About 300 calories per serving.
Start to serve time: 10 minutes.

CHOCOLATE CHEESE PIE

1 9-inch graham
* cracker crust*
1 6-oz. package
* semi-sweet*
* chocolate morsels*
2 8-oz. packages
* cream cheese,*
* softened*
1 14-oz. can
* sweetened*
* condensed*
* milk*
1 teaspoon vanilla
2 eggs, separated

Melt chocolate in top of double boiler. Beat cream cheese with condensed milk, vanilla, and egg yolks until smooth. Beat in chocolate. Beat egg whites until stiff; fold chocolate mixture in gently. Pour into crust and refrigerate until ready to serve.

Serves 12. About 450 calories per serving.
Preparation time: 10 minutes; Chill time: 1/2 hour or more.

DO-IT-ITSELF PIE

1/2 cup coconut
1/2 cup sugar
1/2 cup biscuit mix
1 teaspoon vanilla
1/4 cup butter or
  margarine
2 cups milk
4 eggs

Preheat oven to 350° F.

Place all ingredients in blender; blend until smooth, about 3 minutes. Pour into greased and floured 9-inch pie plate. Bake 45 minutes. Chill until cool.

Serves 8. About 228 calories per serving.
Start to serve time: 50 minutes.

EASY CHEESEY PIE

1 9-inch graham
  cracker crust
1 8-oz. package
  cream cheese,
  softened
1 cup confectioners
  sugar, sifted
1 teaspoon lemon
  juice
1 cup heavy cream,
  whipped

Beat cream cheese with sugar and lemon juice until light and fluffy. Fold into whipped cream. Pour into pie crust and chill.

Serves 8. About 400 calories per serving.
Preparation time: 8 minutes; Chill time: 1 hour or more.

This is one of the lightest, most delicious cheese pies ever. Sprinkle a few fresh berries on top to make it pretty.

NO-BAKE CHEESE "PIE"

1 envelope unflavored gelatin
1/4 cup cold water
1/4 cup hot water
1 teaspoon grated lemon or orange rind
1 tablespoon honey
1 cup unsweetened pineapple juice
1 cup whipped cottage cheese
freshly grated coconut

Soften gelatin in cold water; dissolve in hot water. Add rind, honey, and pineapple juice; fold in cottage cheese. (To whip cottage cheese, put in the blender with a couple of table-spoons of juice and blend on high speed until smooth.)

Lightly oil a 9-inch pie plate. Sprinkle coconut over sides and bottom. Pour in cheese mixture. Chill until set, about an hour.

Serves 6. About 65 calories per serving.
Preparation time: 10 minutes; Chill time: 1 hour.

This has a really creamy and delicious texture and a scrumptious, not-too-sweet taste.

QUICK STRAWBERRY PIE

1 9-inch graham cracker crust
2 10-oz. packages frozen strawberries, thawed
1 package unflavored gelatin
1/3 cup lemon juice
2 egg whites

Drain strawberries; add gelatin to juice and cook over low heat until dissolved. Add lemon juice. Refrigerate until mixture drops in mounds from a spoon.

Beat gelatin mixture and egg whites until light and fluffy; fold in strawberries. Pile into pie crust. Refrigerate.

Serves 8. About 160 calories per serving.
Preparation time: 1/2 hour; Chill time: 1 hour or more.

YOU-WON'T-BELIEVE-WHAT'S-IN-THIS PIE

*1 9-inch graham
    cracker crust*
*6 oz. semi-sweet
    chocolate morsels*
*1 cup shredded
    coconut*
1/2 cup raisins
*1/2 cup chopped
    walnuts*
*1/2 cup condensed
    milk*

Preheat oven to 350°F.

Chill crust or bake for 10 minutes before using. Cover bottom with chocolate chips, then add layers of coconut, raisins, and walnuts. Sprinkle with condensed milk and bake at 350°F. for about 15 or 20 minutes, until the chocolate has melted and all the ingredients have sort of glopped together.

Serves 8. About 450 calories per serving.
Start to serve time: 20 minutes.

The first time I tasted this, I didn't believe what was in it. All the measurements are approximate — use more of what you like most, and as long as the chocolate is on the bottom and the condensed milk is on top, the order in the middle doesn't matter.

MARIA'S NO-BAKE CHOCOLATE COOKIES

1/2 cup milk
*1/4 cup butter or
    margarine*
*1/2 cup unsweetened
    cocoa*
2 cups sugar
1 teaspoon vanilla
*1/2 cup chunky
    peanut butter*
2-1/2 cups quick oats

Put milk, butter or margarine, cocoa, and sugar into a saucepan; bring to a boil, stirring to dissolve sugar. Remove from heat and stir in rest of ingredients. Drop by teaspoonsful onto wax paper; let set about half an hour.

Makes 4 dozen. About 60 calories each.
Preparation time: 10 minutes; Set time: 1/2 hour.

What more can I say — except that these have a mysterious way of disappearing about as fast as you spoon them out.

MUNCHIES

1 6-oz. package
  semi-sweet chocolate
  morsels
2 cups corn flakes,
  crushed
1/2 cup dry roasted
  peanuts
1 teaspoon vanilla

Melt chocolate over hot water; stir in rest of ingredients until well mixed. Drop by teaspoonsful onto waxed paper and let cool.

Makes about 3 dozen. About 68 calories each.

Start to serve time: 1/2 hour.

Someone suggested substituting the noodles you get in Chinese restaurants for the corn flakes. If you try it, and like it, let me know.

DESSERTS FOR DINNER

7

Did you ever consider eating dessert for dinner? Not instead of dinner, but as dinner, a sort of total meal rolled into one. Most obvious would be an omelet filled with something wonderful and sweet—jam, fresh fruit, or even ice cream. But think about a luscious fruit salad, topped with a sweet and creamy dressing. Or French toast, waffles, pancakes, blintzes, or fritters. The opportunities are endless—nutritious, easy, fast, and certainly different from the usual dinner menu.

AN OMELET FOR DINNER AND DESSERT

Everybody has a favorite omelet recipe, whether it's scrambled eggs with a French accent or an expertly flipped masterpiece perfected by hours of practice. Use your special favorite or try mine:

2 eggs, separated
2 tablespoons milk or
  fruit juice
1/2 teaspoon baking
  powder
1 tablespoon sugar

Beat the egg yolks with the milk or juice and baking powder. Beat the whites, in a separate bowl, until they're stiff; gently fold in the yolk mixture. Pour into a skillet in which you've melted 1 tablespoon of butter until it's bubbly; cover, and cook until puffed and done.

That's the dinner part. For the dessert part, spread the top (or, if you've made a more traditional omelet that will fold, spread one half) with jelly, jam, preserves, or puréed fruit. Sprinkle with confectioners sugar and, *voilá*, it's a two-course meal rolled into one.

Serves 1. About 250–300 calories.
Start to serve time: 10-15 minutes.

ORANGE EGGS

2 eggs
3/4 cup orange juice
dash lemon juice

Put all ingredients in the blender with a little bit of crushed ice. Blend until smooth, and then scramble in butter.

Serves 1. About 250 calories.
Start to serve time: 10 minutes.

MELON SALAD

3 cups assorted melon
  chunks
1 grapefruit, peeled
  and sectioned

Combine all ingredients; serve with Piquant Dressing (page 117).

Serves 4. About 100 calories per serving.
Start to serve time: 5 minutes.

FRUIT SALAD SUPREME

1 pineapple
1 orange, peeled and
  sectioned
1 cup strawberries,
  sliced
1/4 cup chopped
  walnuts

Peel pineapple; cut into chunks. Combine with orange, strawberries, and walnuts. Serve with Cream Cheese and Orange Dressing (page 117).

Serves 4. About 65 calories per serving, without dressing.
Start to serve time: 10 minutes.

BANANA BOWL

2 bananas, peeled and
  sliced
2 apples, cored and
  cut in eighths
1/2 cup sliced peaches
1/2 cup sliced pears
1/2 cup seedless grapes

Combine all ingredients in large bowl. Serve with Polynesian or Yogurt Dressing (page 117, 118).

Serves 4–6. About 100 calories per serving, without dressing.
Start to serve time: 6 minutes.

APPLE MERINGUE SOUFFLÉ

2 egg whites, beaten
  to stiff peaks
2/3 cup grated apple

Preheat oven to 350° F.

Fold the stiffly beaten egg whites into the grated apple. Pour into a well-greased 1-quart soufflé dish sprinkled with sugar, and bake 35 minutes. Sprinkle with sugar before serving.

Serves 2. About 60 calories per serving.
Preparation time: 4 minutes; Baking time: 35 minutes.

BASIC SOUFFLÉ

1 tablespoon butter
2 tablespoons flour
1/3 cup hot milk
2 eggs, separated,
  plus 1 extra egg
  white
2 tablespoons sugar
1/2 teaspoon vanilla
1/2 teaspoon almond
  extract
dash salt

Preheat oven to 325° F.

Blend flour and butter in top of double boiler; add milk and cook, beating with a wire whisk, until thick. Beat the egg yolks with 1 tablespoon of the sugar and add to the milk mixture. Add the vanilla and almond extracts, stir well, and cool.

Beat the whites with a dash of salt until soft peaks form; add the remaining sugar and beat until stiff. Fold into the yolk and milk mixture. Pour into a 1-quart soufflé dish, well-buttered, then sprinkle with sugar. Bake 1 hour, or until firm, with soufflé dish set in larger pan of hot water. The best way to tell whether your soufflé is done is to quickly stick a knife into the center. If it comes out clean, the soufflé has cooked through.

Serves 2. About 350 calories per serving.

Preparation time: 10 minutes; Baking time: 1 hour.

This soufflé lends itself to endless variations:

Add 2 squares of unsweetened chocolate to the milk mixture before adding the yolks, and have Chocolate Soufflé.

Instead of milk, use half coffee and half milk, or one third cream and two thirds coffee, and have Mocha Soufflé.

Add 1/4 cup chopped walnuts, folded in with the egg whites, and have Walnut Soufflé.

Put 1 cup sliced raspberries or strawberries that have been soaked in 1/4 cup orange juice and 1/4 cup Kirsch, and then drained, on the bottom of the soufflé dish, then pour the basic mixture over them. *Voilà:* Raspberry or Strawberry Soufflé.

CHOCOLATE SOUFFLÉ

1/2 cup strong coffee
2 squares unsweetened
chocolate
1/2 cup milk
1/3 cup sugar
1/3 cup flour
1/4 teaspoon salt
4 eggs, separated
1 teaspoon vanilla
1/4 teaspoon almond
extract

Preheat oven to 425° F.

Melt coffee and chocolate in top of double boiler; beat until smooth. Stir milk into sugar, flour, and salt, and add to the chocolate. Cook, stirring, until smooth and thick. Remove from heat and beat again until smooth (this gets very, very thick). Add the yolks, one at a time, beating after each addition. Let stand, covered, until ready to fold into the egg whites.

Beat the whites until soft peaks form, gradually, beating until stiff. Fold in chocolate and the vanilla and almond extracts. Pour into a greased and sugared 1-1/2 quart soufflé dish. Bake about 25 minutes, or until knife stuck in center comes out clean (check at 22 minutes, as it could be done by then).

Serves 4. About 300 calories per serving.

Preparation time: 10 minutes; Baking time: 25 minutes.

This is the true chocolate lovers' soufflé — rich, not-too-sweet, and delicious.

COLD ORANGE SOUFFLÉ

3/4 cup sugar
1 tablespoon orange
  rind
1/4 cup water
6 egg yolks
1/3 cup Grand
  Marnier
2-3/4 cups heavy
  cream, whipped

Combine sugar, rind, and water in saucepan and simmer, stirring to dissolve sugar, for 10 minutes or until syrupy. Beat yolks slightly in a large bowl; add syrup in a steady stream, beating at high speed until it falls in ribbons from the beater. Beat in liqueur until thick. Fold gently but thoroughly into cream. Pour into a 2-quart soufflé dish and freeze 2 hours.

Serves 8. About 400 calories per serving.
Preparation time: 20 minutes; Freeze time: 2 hours.

GRAND MARNIER SOUFFLÉ

6 egg whites
2 cups milk
3/4 cup sugar
1/4 cup butter
1/3 cup flour
1/4 cup Grand
  Marnier
4 egg yolks

Preheat oven to 400°F.

Beat egg whites until stiff.

Bring milk and sugar just to the boil, stirring to dissolve sugar. Melt butter; add flour, stirring until blended, and add to milk. Cook, stirring, until thick and smooth. Remove from heat and after a few seconds, add Grand Marnier, stirring to blend well.

Beat yolks until thick and lemon-colored; add to milk mixture. Beat egg whites until stiff and fold into yolk mixture. Pour into greased and sugared 2-quart soufflé dish, and bake 30 minutes (check at 20 or 25 minutes, with the old knife trick).

Preparation time: 15 minutes; Baking time: 1/2 hour.

This is a classic soufflé, with an almost infinite number of "true" versions. This is my favorite, but I make no claims as to its authenticity. As with any soufflé, it takes a bit of time and practice to do correctly, but it's well worth it in the end.

LEMON SOUFFLÉ

4 egg whites
1/3 cup sugar
4 egg yolks
1/3 cup sugar
grated rind and juice
of one lemon
1/4 cup chopped
walnuts

Preheat oven to 350°F.

Beat whites until soft peaks form; add 1/3 cup sugar gradually, beating until stiff. In a separate bowl, beat yolks until thick; beat in the remaining 1/3 cup sugar. Stir in rind, juice, and nuts; fold in whites. Pour into 1-1/2 quart soufflé dish and bake 40 minutes.

Serves 4. 300 calories per serving.
Preparation time: 7 minutes; Baking time: 40 minutes.

As with all soufflés, serve immediately or it will collapse (and taste fine, but look strange). You can prepare the yolk mixture ahead and add egg whites at the last minute.

For a little chewier version of a lemon soufflé, blend 2 tablespoons flour and 1 tablespoon butter in a saucepan, add 1/2 cup milk, and stir and cook until thick. Cool and then add the yolk mixture from above and fold the whole thing into the egg whites. Bake 40 minutes in a 1-1/2 quart soufflé dish with a 6-inch collar of waxed paper around it.

NOT-QUITE-A-SOUFFLÉ

2 egg yolks
1/4 cup sifted
* confectioners sugar*
1/2 teaspoon vanilla
4 egg whites
1 tablespoon sugar
grated rind of 1
* orange or lemon*

Preheat oven to 300° F.

Beat yolks until light; beat in confectioners sugar and vanilla. Beat whites until stiff; beat in sugar and rind. Fold whites into yolks. Pile the mixture on a well-greased, heat-proof oval or round platter, and smooth it down into a neat but high mound. Cut a lengthwise groove down the center, and bake for 30 minutes, or until golden.

Serves 2. About 186 calories per serving.
Preparation time: 5 minutes; Baking time: 1/2 hour.

This is almost an omelet and almost a soufflé. It's sweet, but not overpowering, and makes a perfect dinner and dessert rolled into one.

PEACH SOUFFLÉ

1 cup peach purée
1-1/2 tablespoons
* lemon juice*
4 egg yolks, well
* beaten*
dash of salt
sugar to taste
4 egg whites, stiffly
* beaten*

Preheat oven to 350° F.

Combine all ingredients except egg whites and stir well. Fold into stiffly beaten whites, and pour into a greased and sugared 1-quart soufflé dish. Bake in a pan of hot water, 30 minutes.

Serves 4. About 100 calories per serving.
Preparation time: 10 minutes; Baking time: 1/2 hour.

You can substitute any fruit purée you like (use baby-food purée, or blend fruit in the blender until smooth), especially whatever is in season.

TOP-OF-THE-STOVE CHOCOLATE SOUFFLÉ

2 squares unsweetened
   chocolate
4 tablespoons sugar
1 cup milk
1/4 teaspoon vanilla
1/4 teaspoon almond
   extract
2 eggs

Combine chocolate, sugar, and milk in the top of a double boiler and heat until chocolate is melted. Add the vanilla and almond extracts, and stir until well-blended. Add the eggs and beat with a rotary beater or wire whisk for about 4 minutes (a little tough on your arms, but an electric mixer is too big). Cover and cook, over hot water, 1/2 hour.

Serves 2. 350 calories per serving.
Start to serve time: 40 minutes.

This has the texture of a soufflé, with a delicious bittersweet taste, but it doesn't rise to great heights as conventional soufflés do. You can serve it hot or cold.

GINGER-MELON SALAD

3 cups honeydew, cut
   into chunks
2 tablespoons lemon
   or lime juice
1/4 teaspoon ground
   ginger
4 teaspoons sugar

Mix lemon juice, ginger, and sugar together; pour over melon chunks. Refrigerate until chilled.

Serves 4. About 60 calories per serving.
Preparation time: 5 minutes; Chill time: 1/2 hour or more.

AMBROSIA

1 11-oz. can
   mandarin orange
   slices
1 13-oz. can
   pineapple chunks
1-1/2 cups miniature
   marshmallows, or
   large ones cut into
   quarters
1 cup grated coconut
1/2 cup heavy cream,
   whipped

Drain the fruits, mix with marshmallows and coconut. Fold into the whipped cream and chill.

Serves 6–8. About 300 calories per serving.
Preparation time: 10 minutes; Chill time: 1/2 hour or more.

Ambrosia is, historically, the food of the gods. But except for the coconut, the specific god-pleasing ingredients are variable. Try adding an apple here, a few grapes there. . . . Here's one variation I like because it's less fattening:

AMBROSIA, TOO

1 lb. applesauce
   (homemade,
   canned, or from
   jar)
2 bananas, sliced
1 11-oz. can mandarin
   orange slices,
   drained
1/2 cup toasted
   almonds
1/2 cup coconut

Combine all ingredients and chill. Serve with whipped cream, sour cream, or yogurt spooned on top.

Serves 6. About 217 calories per serving.
Preparation time: 5 minutes; Chill time: 1/2 hour or more.

FRENCH TOAST

If you've always thought French toast was a breakfast treat, you're in for a big surprise. It makes a delicious dinner-dessert combo, in no time at all.

1 egg
1/2 cup milk
dash of salt
1/2 teaspoon vanilla
or almond extract
4 slices bread (white,
French, Italian,
raisin, Challah —
almost any kind
will do, and the
older, the better)

Beat eggs, milk, salt, and extract together; dip each slice of bread into the mixture and fry in a lightly buttered, hot skillet, until golden on both sides.

Here's the dessert touch: sprinkle the French toast with a mixture of sugar and cinnamon, then top with jam, jelly, preserves, fresh or frozen fruit, applesauce, maple syrup, bananas and sour cream, or just about anything that tastes good to you.

Serves 2. About 200 calories per serving.
Start to serve time: 10 minutes.

TOAST FOR DESSERT

Don't let this fool you, it's not just toast, it's TOAST, topped with a delicious assortment that takes it well out of the breakfast-food category.

Spread toasted, sliced bread with any one of the following and slip under the broiler for a few minutes until glazed.

Maple Toast:

Mix butter with maple syrup and cinnamon to a spreadable consistency.

Cinnamon Toast:

Butter toast; top with apple slices; sprinkle with cinnamon sugar.

Surprise:

Butter toast; sprinkle with a mixture of grated orange or lemon rind, orange juice, and sugar.

Sweet Butter Toast:

Combine a little honey with butter and a spoonful of cream; spread on toast and glaze.

Serves as many as you like. About 150 calories per slice.

Start to serve time: 5 minutes each.

WAFFLES WITH A KICK

8 *frozen waffles*
1 *large can dark sweet*
  cherries, pitted
2 *tablespoons rum*
1/2 *teaspoon*
  cinnamon
1/2 *cup sour cream*
  or whipped cream

Toast waffles according to directions. Combine cherries, rum, and cinnamon; top each waffle with cherry mixture. Serve topped with sour cream or whipped cream.

Serves 8. 175 calories per serving.

Start to serve time: 5 minutes.

BELGIAN WAFFLES, AMERICAN STYLE

6 *frozen waffles*
1 *cup heavy cream*
2 *tablespoons sugar*
1 *teaspoon vanilla*
  extract
1 *cup fresh, or 1*
  16-oz. package
  frozen, sliced
  strawberries

Toast waffles according to directions. Whip cream with sugar and vanilla, fold in strawberries. Top each waffle with whipped cream mixture; sprinkle with confectioners sugar, if desired.

Serves 6. 220 calories per serving.

Start to serve time: 8 minutes.

This can be made ahead and refrigerated, if you like.

PANCAKES

Everyone has his/her own favorite way to make pancakes, the easiest being to add eggs and milk to prepackaged ingredients. That's just fine, and saves a lot of sifting and preparation. To make pancakes a dessert and dinner all-in-one, to the basic recipe add:

blueberries

thinly sliced apples

thinly sliced bananas

strawberries

peaches, nectarines, pears, or any fruit

currants or raisins

Then proceed as usual. If you want to be really fancy, pour a little batter on the griddle or pan, add a little fruit, then a little more batter, and brown until golden, then flip. Serve sprinkled with powdered sugar.

One plain pancake has about 65 calories; the fruit, unless heavily sugared, adds very little.

Start to serve time: 15 minutes.

COTTAGE CHEESE PANCAKES

*1 cup creamed
  cottage cheese
2 eggs, lightly beaten
1 tablespoon sugar
1/4 cup sifted flour
1/8 teaspoon salt*

Put the cottage cheese and eggs in a blender, and blend at high speed until smooth. Add the rest of the ingredients and blend on low speed until just mixed. Drop by tablespoonsful on hot griddle or skillet. Serve with fresh strawberries or preserves.

Serves 4-6. About 200 calories each.

Start to serve time: 15 minutes.

BAKED PANCAKES

2 teaspoons butter
1 egg
dash of salt
3 tablespoons flour
3 tablespoons milk
grated lemon or
   orange rind

Preheat oven to 450°F.

Grease a small skillet with butter. Beat all ingredients together until smooth, or put in blender until thoroughly combined and smooth. Pour the batter into the skillet and bake at 450°F. for 10 minutes; reduce heat to 400°F. for 5 minutes; reduce to 350°F. for additional 5 to 10 minutes. Top with jelly, fresh fruit, or cinnamon sugar. You can also make this pancake on top of the stove: Melt the butter in the skillet, pour in the batter, and cook, partially covered over low heat, for 5 to 7 minutes.

Serves 1. About 350 calories.
Start to serve time: 20 minutes.

SOME SORT OF A PANCAKE

2 eggs, separated
4 tablespoons sugar
1 tablespoon flour
2 tablespoons butter
   or margarine
confectioners sugar

Preheat oven to 325°F.

Beat egg whites until frothy; add sugar and beat until stiff. Beat yolks with flour until thick; fold in whites.

Melt butter in an ovenproof frying pan. Spoon eggs into hot butter in four portions. Cook 1 minute and remove to preheated oven. Bake for about 7 minutes, or until golden brown. Serve sprinkled with confectioners sugar.

Serves 4. About 140 calories per serving.
Start to serve time: 15 minutes.

This is truly delicious, and worth all the steps it takes to get there.

INSTANT "BLINTZ"

4 slices white bread
3/4 cup cottage
cheese
1 egg yolk
1 teaspoon sugar
1/4 teaspoon
cinnamon
1/4 cup raisins

Trim crusts from white bread; roll thin with rolling pin. Put cottage cheese in blender with egg yolk and sugar; blend until smooth. Soak raisins in hot water for ten minutes (while you're doing everything else), add to cheese mixture with cinnamon, and mix well.

Put about 2 tablespoons of cheese mixture on each slice of bread; roll up as you would jelly roll. Melt butter in a skillet and saute "blintzes" until golden.

Makes 4. About 100 calories each.
Start to serve time: 15–20 minutes.

Not exactly like mother used to make, but every bit as good.

APRICOT FRITTERS

1-1/4 cups flour
1/2 teaspoon baking
*   powder*
1 teaspoon sugar
1/2 teaspoon salt
1 egg
1/2 cup milk
1/2 tablespoon butter
apricots

Mix dry ingredients; beat egg; add milk and melted butter; mix with dry ingredients into stiff batter. Dip each apricot into batter and deep fry until golden brown.

Serves 5. About 225 calories per serving.

Start to serve time: 10-15 minutes.

Peaches or bananas can be substituted for apricots if you prefer them.

BATTERED BERRIES

1 cup blueberries,
*   raspberries, or*
*   strawberries*
7 teaspoons sugar
1 teaspoon cognac
1/2 cup sifted flour
1/8 cup sugar
1/4 cup milk
3 tablespoons sweet
*   sherry*
1 egg, beaten
oil for deep frying
1/4 cup confectioners
*   sugar sifted with*
*   1/2 teaspoon*
*   cinnamon*

Sprinkle berries with sugar and cognac, and let stand, covered, for about half an hour. Drain well before adding to the batter. Fresh berries are naturally, the best, but frozen ones, not in syrup, will work well, also.

Sift flour and sugar together; add milk, sherry, and eggs, beating until very smooth. Add berries, and coat well.

Heat oil to about 370°F. Drop the batter by tablespoons into the hot oil, and fry until golden brown. Drain on paper towels; sprinkle with cinnamon sugar before serving.

Makes 8. About 125 calories each.

Start to serve time: 45 minutes.

This works equally as well with bananas (let two bananas, cut first crosswise, then lengthwise, stand for half an hour sprinkled with 1/8 cup sugar, 1 teaspoon lemon juice, 1 teaspoon cognac); fresh sweet cherries (pitted, please); or thinly sliced, peeled, and cored apples that have been allowed to stand sprinkled with the same proportions of sugar and cognac, plus 1/2 teaspoon of cinnamon. They go fast, so make plenty.

DESSERTS
YOU CAN DRINK

8

Why not drink dessert? It could be a delightful change and a challenging experience. Milk shakes, ice cream sodas, floats, and even fruit-flavored eggnogs qualify as both beverages and desserts. They're easy to do, and combine all the best ingredients: milk, eggs, fruit, and ice cream. What's more, they're fun to create and even more fun to drink.

DESSERTS TO DRINK

Ice Cream Sodas

For each serving, mix together, either in a blender for a real whipped texture or in the serving glass itself, 1/4 cup of milk and 2 or 3 tablespoons of crushed or puréed fruit or flavored syrup. Add 2 scoops of ice cream, and fill the glass with ginger ale or any carbonated soda.

Some combinations I like:

chocolate syrup and vanilla, chocolate, coffee, or butter-almond ice cream

crushed strawberries and vanilla or strawberry ice cream

vanilla extract and almost any flavor ice cream

almond extract and butter-almond or chocolate ice cream or, instead of any flavoring, experiment with cola, black cherry soda, or any flavor fruit soda with a complementary sherbet.

This will have between 350 and 400 calories.

Start to serve time: 5-7 minutes each.

Milk Shakes

This works best in the blender: Mix one cup milk with one scoop of ice cream. You can add any flavorings you want — strawberries, instant coffee, chocolate syrup, mashed bananas — and vary the ice cream flavors accordingly. Or, instead of milk, try orange juice, coffee, or buttermilk.

Start to serve time: 5-7 minutes each.

Eggnogs

In a blender or a tall jar, per serving, combine 1 egg, 1 cup milk, 2 teaspoons sugar, a dash of vanilla, and shake or blend well. For variety, add some frozen fruit-juice concentrate; regular fruit juice; a scoop of ice cream; maple syrup; or any other flavoring you think you might like.

Plain, this has about 164 calories per glass; add 200 calories for a scoop of ice cream, and between 25 and 50 for various flavorings.

Start to serve time: 5-7 minutes each.

FREEZES AND FROSTEDS

Here again, a blender works best, although you can shake up the ingredients reasonably well in a jar or mix all together with an electric mixer. You can make crushed ice in your blender if, in the manufacturer's directions, it tells you you can. Otherwise, put ice cubes in a double plastic bag and smash well with a hammer.

Basically, per serving, you'll need 1/2 cup liquid — milk or fruit juice — 1/2 cup crushed ice, 1/2 cup crushed or mashed fruit or fruit purée, a little sugar or honey to taste, and a dash of flavoring — vanilla, almond, or liqueur. Mix or blend them all together well, until the ice is not quite liquified, and drink up. Try mashed bananas, raspberries, apricots, strawberries;

you can add some ice cream if you like, which makes it more like an ice milk shake.

Figure about 200 calories per glassful, more if you add ice cream or sherbet.

With all these dessert drinks, use your imagination. Puréed baby foods work especially well if you don't have a blender, as you don't have to mash or sieve fruit by hand. Canned or frozen fruit, well drained, gives you a wide range. Try mixing fruit juices instead of using just one; try some different flavors like cranberry juice or apple juice; apricot or peach nectar, or frozen lemonade or limeade concentrate. Anything goes, and you'll be pleasantly surprised at the result. My only bad experience came when I mixed peppermint ice cream with strawberry soda — it tasted as sickening as it sounds.

SAUCES FOR ICE CREAM, FRUIT, AND CAKE

9

Now it's time for you to become the saucerer's apprentice. A few little tricks with chocolate, some magical doings with whipped cream, and — presto! — you've changed a plain old piece of cake into a wondrous dessert, in about as much time as it takes to say abracadabra.

Almost anything is a sauce as long as you can pour or spoon it over something. Even whipped cream takes on new dimensions when it's subtly flavored with a little liqueur, fruit purée, or extract. A bowl of tantalizing fresh fruit becomes irresistible when you serve it with a few easy fondue sauces for dipping. And as wonderful as ice cream is, dressed up with a special sauce, it's fantastic.

Most of these sauces and toppings can be stored in the refrigerator for a few days; some you may have to reheat to bring them back to their original pourable consistency. But make more than you immediately need — tomorrow's another day and another dessert.

COOKING HINTS

Be wise in choosing which sauce goes over what dessert. Too many sweet tastes at once spoil a good thing; the same is true for too much blandness.

If you're using cornstarch or flour as a thickener, dissolve it first in a little cold water until it is smooth. Otherwise, you'll wind up with lumpy sauce.

Remember to fold, not beat, ingredients into whipped cream or egg whites, in order to keep the texture of the finished dessert light and airy.

When you're boiling sugar and water to make a syrup, keep a close watch on it — you don't want the sugar to crystallize. Then it's a mess to clean up and certainly useless for your recipe.

CHANTILLY SAUCE

1/2 cup heavy cream
2 tablespoons powdered sugar
1 tablespoon cognac, fruit-flavored brandy, or flavored liqueur

Whip cream with sugar and flavoring.

Makes about 1 cup. About 35 calories per tablespoon.
Start to serve time: 4–5 minutes.

This is particularly terrific over fresh berries.

QUICK MELBA SAUCE

1/4 cup raspberry jam or red currant jelly
1 cup raspberries, puréed

Melt jam over low heat; mix with puréed raspberries.

Makes about 1 cup. About 20 calories per tablespoon.
Start to serve time: 4 minutes.

Spoon over a peach half filled with vanilla ice cream and you have instant Peach Melba.

WHIPPED CUSTARD CREAM SAUCE

2 egg yolks
1/3 cup sugar
1/3 cup melted butter
1 tablespoon grated
  lemon or orange
  rind
2 tablespoons lemon
  or orange juice
1/2 cup heavy cream,
  whipped

Beat yolks until thick, gradually adding the sugar. Blend in butter, rind, and juice; mix until smooth. Fold into whipped cream.

Makes 1-1/2 cups. About 55 calories per tablespoon.

Start to serve time: 10 minutes.

COOKED VANILLA SAUCE

1 cup brown sugar,
  firmly packed
1 cup boiling water
1 tablespoon
  cornstarch mixed
  with 2 tablespoons
  water until smooth
4 tablespoons butter
1 teaspoon vanilla

Stir sugar into water until dissolved; add cornstarch mix, and cook until thick. Add butter and vanilla and combine well.

Makes 2 cups. About 36 calories per tablespoon.

Start to serve time: 8 minutes.

Good warm or cold, over cake or fruit.

BRANDIED BUTTER SAUCE

1/2 cup butter or
  margarine, softened
2 tablespoons heavy
  cream
2 tablespoons brandy
1-1/2 to 2 cups
  confectioners sugar,
  sifted

With an electric mixer, blend butter or margarine with cream until light and fluffy. Add brandy and sugar alternately, beating well after each addition. Beat at high speed about 1 minute longer. Serve immediately or chill.

Makes 1-3/4 cups. About 85 calories per tablespoon.

Start to serve time: 4 minutes.

As I like this less sweet, I use less sugar. If you have a really insatiable sweet tooth, use the full two cups. This is particularly good over something warm, like "Apple Pudding" (page 16).

BERRY SAUCE

1 8-oz. package cream cheese, softened and cut up into cubes
1 cup sour cream
1/8 teaspoon salt
1/4 cup honey

With an electric mixer, cream cheese until smooth; gradually add sour cream, beating well. Add salt, beat again; gradually add honey until it's all smooth and creamy.

Makes 2 cups. About 45 calories per tablespoon.
Start to serve time: 5 minutes.

This is called BERRY SAUCE because it goes so well with berries.

SURPRISE FUDGE SAUCE

3/4 cup hot cream
4 oz. sweet chocolate, broken into small pieces
4 cups miniature marshmallows

Place all ingredients in a blender and blend at high speed until smooth.

Makes 1-1/2 cups. About 88 calories per tablespoon.
Start to serve time: 4 minutes.

Yummy over coffee ice cream.

BUTTERSCOTCH SAUCE

*2 tablespoons butter
  or margarine,
  softened
3/4 cup brown sugar,
  firmly packed
1/2 cup granulated
  sugar
1 cup evaporated milk
1 teaspoon vanilla*

With an electric mixer, beat butter or margarine with brown and granulated sugar until well combined. Gradually add the rest of the ingredients, beating until smooth.

Makes 1-1/2 cups. About 45 calories per tablespoon.

Start to serve time: 7 minutes.

NUTSY SAUCE

*1 cup slivered
  almonds, chopped
  walnuts, or chopped
  pecans
1 tablespoon butter
  or margarine
1-1/4 cups honey*

Mix nuts with butter in a small heatproof dish and toast in the oven until golden. Place the nuts and honey in a blender, and blend at high speed until well combined and nuts are chopped. Serve as is or cool.

Makes 1-1/2 cups. About 120 calories per tablespoon.

Start to serve time: 17 minutes.

Try this mixed into ice cream or pudding, yogurt or whipped cream, as well as on top of things.

BANANAS 'N CREAM

*1 very ripe banana
1 cup sour cream
2 tablespoons honey*

Mash banana till smooth; combine with sour cream and honey.

Makes 1-1/2 cups. About 25 calories per tablespoon.

Start to serve time: 4 minutes.

APRICOTS AND HONEY SAUCE

*1 cup baby food
  apricot purée*
1/4 cup honey
*1/2 cup heavy cream,
  whipped*

Beat honey into apricot purée until smooth and well combined. Fold into whipped cream.

Makes 1-1/2 cups. About 44 calories per tablespoon.

Start to serve time: 5 minutes.

FAST AND EASY BLUEBERRY SAUCE

*1 10-oz. package
  frozen, unsweetened
  blueberries, or 1 cup
  fresh*
*1/4 cup brown sugar,
  firmly packed*
*1 tablespoon orange
  juice*
*1/4 teaspoon
  cinnamon*

Cook all ingredients together over medium heat until hot and bubbly. Stir occasionally. Refrigerate until ready to use.

Makes 1-1/2 cups. About 20 calories per tablespoon.

Preparation time: 6 minutes; Chill time: 1/2 hour or more.

Super over pound cake slices or ice cream.

HOTSY TOTSY FRUIT SAUCE

*1 8-3/4 oz. can
  peaches, drained
1 10-oz. can crushed
  pineapple, drained
1 10-oz. can plums,
  drained
2 tablespoons brown
  sugar
1 tablespoon orange
  juice
1 teaspoon butter or
  margarine
1/4 teaspoon
  cinnamon*

Place well-drained fruits in large saucepan; add other in-gredients. Cook until fruit is very hot, stirring and basting gently with the sauce that it makes.

Serves 6. About 120 calories per serving.
Start to serve time: 8 minutes.

This does wonders for plain cake or ice cream, or both. Use any combination of fruits you like or happen to have around; 1 large can of fruit cocktail works, too.

FLAMING WALNUT SAUCE

*1-1/2 cups chopped
  walnuts
1/2 cup butter or
  margarine
1 cup brown sugar,
  firmly packed
1 tablespoon grated
  orange rind
1/4 cup heated brandy*

Saute walnuts in butter until lightly browned, about 5 minutes. Add brown sugar and orange rind and stir, over low heat, until sugar is melted, and begins to bubble. Add heated brandy, and let it warm further, without stirring. Ignite and pour over fruit or ice cream.

Makes 2 cups. About 75 calories per tablespoon.
Start to serve time: 15 minutes.

Heat the brandy in a small saucepan just before pouring it into the sauce. Then you'll have a really impressive flambée.

DRESSINGS FOR FRESH FRUIT SALADS

Piquant Dressing

1/2 cup lemon juice
1/3 cup sugar
1/4 cup dry sherry
1/4 teaspoon salt

Combine all ingredients well in a blender, jar, or mixing bowl.

Makes 3/4 cup. About 30 calories per tablespoon.
Start to serve time: 4 minutes.

Polynesian Dressing

1 cup sour cream
2 tablespoons brown
sugar
2 tablespoons orange
juice

Combine all ingredients well.

Makes 1 cup. About 50 calories per tablespoon.
Start to serve time: 3 minutes.

Strawberry Dressing

1/2 cup strawberries
1 cup sour cream or
yogurt
1 tablespoon brown
sugar
1 tablespoon rum
1 banana, sliced
dash of ginger

Combine all ingredients in a blender until smooth.

Makes 2 cups. About 25 calories per tablespoon.
Start to serve time: 5 minutes.

Cream Cheese and Orange Dressing

1 8-oz. package cream
cheese, softened
1/4 cup orange juice
1 tablespoon grated
orange peel
dash of salt
1/2 cup heavy cream,
whipped

Beat cream cheese with orange juice, salt, and peel until light and fluffy. Fold into whipped cream.

Makes 2 cups. About 45 calories per tablespoon.
Start to serve time: 10 minutes.

Yogurt Dressing

1 cup plain yogurt
1/4 cup lemon juice
1/2 cup salad oil
1 tablespoon wheat germ
2 teaspoons honey
raisins

Put all ingredients except raisins in blender and blend on high speed until smooth. Add raisins.

Makes 2 cups. About 20 calories per tablespoon.
Start to serve time: 5 minutes.

Add a handful of chopped nuts for a delicious variation.

FRUIT FONDUE

Just heap a platter full of fruit: whole strawberries, sliced apples, pears, peaches, bananas, pineapple — even add some chunks of plain cake — and serve with any one or a combination of the sauces below. Everybody dips for himself.

Raspberry Dip

1 10-oz. package frozen raspberries, thawed and drained
1 tablespoon sugar
4-oz. cream cheese, softened

Blend sugar and raspberries in a blender until smooth. If the seeds bother you, push through a sieve before adding to the cream cheese; if they don't, just beat the cream cheese with an electric mixer until smooth, and gradually beat in the raspberries.

Serves 6. About 180 calories (without fruit) per serving.
Start to serve time: 8 minutes.

Double Dip

1 cup cream
1/4 cup butter or
  margarine
3/4 cup brown sugar,
  firmly packed
1/4 cup granulated
  sugar
dash of salt
dash of cinnamon

Bring all ingredients to a boil in a heavy pot; boil until the mixture drops in ribbons from the spoon. Pour into a fondue pot and keep on low heat on fondue stand. Dip fruit into sauce, then into a bowl of chopped nuts.

Serves 6. About 175 calories per serving (without fruit).
Start to serve time: 15 minutes.

Instant Caramel Dip

24 caramels
2 tablespoons butter
  or margarine
2 tablespoons water
2 tablespoons whiskey

Combine all ingredients over low heat until melted; pour into fondue pot and keep hot while guests dip.

Makes 1 cup. About 65 calories per tablespoon.
Start to serve time: 8 minutes.

Syrup Dip

2/3 cup sugar
1/4 cup water
1 ounce Kirsch

Cook sugar and water at boil until a half-teaspoonful forms a soft ball when dropped into cold water. Add Kirsch; pour into fondue pot and keep warm.

Makes 1/2 cup. 75 calories per tablespoon.
Start to serve time: 10 minutes.

Mint Dip

3/4 cup water
1/2 cup water
3 tablespoons lemon
  juice
1/4 cup fresh mint
  leaves, chopped

Bring water and sugar to a boil; cook for about 6 minutes or until syrupy. Add mint leaves and let cool. Remove mint, add lemon juice, and chill until ready to serve.

Serves 6. 65 calories per serving.
Preparation time: 14 minutes; Chill time: 1/2 hour or more.

This does not work with dried mint, so wait until your garden is in bloom or fresh mint is available at the market.

Yogurt Dip

1 cup plain yogurt
1 tablespoon lime
  juice
4 tablespoons honey

Mix all ingredients together until well blended.

Serves 6. About 50 calories per serving.
Start to serve time: 5 minutes.

Cocamon Dip

3/4 cup sugar
2-1/2 tablespoons
  cocoa
1 tablespoon
  cinnamon
1/4 cup shredded
  coconut

Mix all ingredients together.

Makes about 1-1/2 cups. About 35 calories per tablespoon.
Start to serve time: 3 minutes.

Strawberry Dip

1 cup strawberry
  yogurt
4 strawberries

Blend in the blender until smooth.

Makes about 1 cup. About 15 calories per tablespoon.
Start to serve time: 3 minutes.

Orange Cream Dip

3/4 cup heavy cream,
  whipped
3 tablespoons
  Cointreau or Grand
  Marnier
1 teaspoon grated
  orange rind
1 teaspoon sugar

Combine all ingredients.

Makes 1-1/2 cups. 35 calories per tablespoon.
Start to serve time: 2 minutes.

FLAVORED WHIPPED CREAM

To one cup of heavy cream, whipped to the soft peak stage, you can add almost anything and go on whipping until stiff. For example:

3 tablespoons confectioners sugar; 1/2 teaspoon vanilla

1/2 cup chopped nuts

1 tablespoon rum or Kirsch, Grand Marnier, brandy, etc.

1/2 cup jam or preserves

1/2 cup fresh, canned or frozen fruit, well drained

1 tablespoon maple syrup

1 teaspoon almond extract

2 tablespoons cocoa plus 3 tablespoons confectioners sugar

2 tablespoons sweetened coffee

2 tablespoons confectioners sugar; 1 teaspoon grated orange or lemon rind; 1 tablespoon orange or lemon juice

These are only suggestions, and my preferences at that. Use your imagination, intuition, and inspiration. Flavored whipped cream is a quick, deliciously gooey way to improve a dessert.

SUPER-DUPER QUICKIES

The recipes in this chapter are for those real lazy days, when you just don't feel like fussing or when you're in a super-duper rush but still want a fantastic dessert to complete your dinner. Or, for that matter, any time at all. Most of them require no cooking, or a truly bare minimum. The total time expended won't be more than 10 minutes — just enough to make them super-quick and super-special.

These recipes will probably take longer to read than they will to make.

Top a baked apple pie with grated sharp Cheddar cheese; bake at 325°F. until cheese melts. Looks good; tastes great.

Top freshly baked or bought brownies with a thin layer of cream cheese softened with a little heavy cream; top with thinly sliced unpeeled apples or peaches. Pretty as a picture.

Toast pound cake slightly. Top with applesauce mixed with a little cinnamon, a dash of nutmeg, brown sugar, and lemon juice. Top with a dollop of whipped cream if you want to be fancy.

Top applesauce with crushed vanilla wafers and a spoonful of flavored whipped cream. A dessert fit for a king.

Alternate layers of sweetened applesauce and vanilla ice cream with quick thawed raspberries or strawberries. It's almost too beautiful to eat.

Slice unpeeled apples into half-inch rings. Spread with preserves, top with whipped cream, sprinkle with toasted coconut. Dee-licious.

Split plain or cinnamon donuts in half, crosswise; spread with chocolate syrup; top with ice cream. The fastest ice cream cake in the West.

Mix a little maple syrup into a cup of yogurt; top with chopped nuts. A surprisingly delicious combination.

Who says shortcake is hard to make? Just top pound cake or angel food cake slices with fresh, frozen, or canned fruit and top with whipped cream. Looks beautiful; tastes grand.

Dip pound cake slices into beaten egg and milk; fry in melted butter until golden. A different kind of French toast, delicious with maple syrup, honey, or cinnamon.

Make equal layers of raspberry sherbet, vanilla ice cream, and Quick Melba Sauce in parfait glasses. Try it with coffee ice cream, too.

Top chilled applesauce with any one of the following: ice cream, sour cream, yogurt, or whipped cream. Sprinkle with cinnamon sugar for an instant and elegant combo.

Spread pound cake slices with butter or margarine; top with a sprinkling of coconut; broil until toasted. Tastes as good as it looks.

Shred two apples and mix with a little honey, a little lemon juice, and some chopped raisins. Serve topped with chopped nuts and toasted coconut. What could be easier?

Slice a banana thinly, crosswise. Divide into two dishes; top with half a scoop each of coffee and chocolate ice creams; sprinkle coffee-flavored liqueur on top. Instantly terrific.

Into one package of any quick-thaw fruit, mix a diced apple. Top with sour cream and sprinkle with cinnamon, or top with whipped cream and chopped nuts. Superb!

Cut brownies into three layers. Spread with your favorite preserves and restack. Cut into thin slices to serve, and pretend it took hours to make.

Spread applesauce in the bottom of a baked pie crust or graham cracker crust. Top with your favorite ice cream and serve right away. A real winner.

Thin two tablespoons of honey with a little whiskey or brandy. Pour over coffee or chocolate ice cream and top with chopped pecans. You'll be nuts over it.

Heat bran muffins in the oven for a few minutes. Top with a mixture of orange juice, sugar, and almond extract. Let it sink in, then eat to your heart's content.

Be an instant pudding enhancer. In a pinch, mix any one of the following into your favorite instant pudding, and eat with gusto:

melted chocolate or chocolate chips
shredded coconut
orange or tangerine sections
fresh or frozen fruit
preserves
crushed peanut brittle
chopped nuts
instant coffee
sherry, rum, or brandy to taste
ice cream
whipped cream
marshmallows
cookie crumbs
fruit cocktail
vanilla, almond, or mint extract
any fruit-flavored brandy or liqueur
maraschino cherries
apple pie or cherry pie filling
You name it!

There are no absolutes when it comes to these desserts; variety is the spice of life. If you haven't got strawberry preserves, don't worry; use whatever you have around. Cookie crumbs of almost any persuasion are interchangeable; use yogurt instead of sour cream or vice versa. If there's really no time to whip your own cream (which takes only five minutes with an electric mixer), the cream in the spray can is my choice for a substitute. "Whipped toppings," frozen or otherwise, are next best; be aware, though, that they contain a lot of chemicals. If you want to be fancy real fast, mix something nutty (peanut butter?) or fruity (crushed pineapple?) into slightly softened vanilla ice cream, and put it back in the freezer until you're ready to serve it. Instant puddings and pie fillings set in five minutes; they may not be a gourmet's choice, but they are fast, and they taste good. Poured into a pie shell and topped with whipped cream, they're as terrific an instant dessert as you're likely to find.

INDEX